GROOVE ESSENTIALS
THE PLAY-ALONG
THE GROOVE ENCYCLOPEDIA
FOR THE 21ST-CENTURY DRUMMER

Handwritten notes:

pas.com

26 Standard American Drum Rudiments

HD1 or HD3
Roland or Yamaha Electric Drum Kit
Mesh head

Trinity Rock and Pop Grade 2 Drums

TOMMY IGOE ▪ VIC FIRTH ▪ HUDSON MUSIC

GROOVE ESSENTIALS
THE PLAY-ALONG

Written by Tommy Igoe

Design—Jo Hay

Editing—Gayle Giese

Notation Engraving—Jack Mansager

Guitars—Kevin Kuhn

Keyboards—Ted Baker and Allen Farnham

Basses—Vashon Johnson

Percussion—Rolando Morales-Matos

Saxophones—Darmon Meader

All songs, bad humor, and unheeded cries for sleep written by Kevin Kuhn, Ted Baker, Vashon Johnson,

Allen Farnham, and Tommy Igoe, except "Endure," written by Tommy Igoe.

All songs © 2004 Deep Rhythm Music.

Recorded, Produced, Engineered, Mixed, Mastered, Massaged, and Buffed to a Nice-Shiny-Glow at

Deep Rhythm Music Studios by Tommy Igoe.

Tommy Igoe plays exclusively:

Vic Firth Sticks, Mallets and Brushes, and other items of Whackery

Yamaha Drums and hardware. I still have my vintage "Yahmee" hardware from the 1980s! Solid as a rock.

Zildjian Round Metal Things—there's a name for them . . . symbol? Simbal? Curse you, short-term memory!

Evans drumheads. Yes, they still make the awesome blue hydraulics!

Latin Percussion, because they really, really needed an Irish/Austrian kid from Jersey to round out their roster.

Rhythm Tech: You know, I always thought rhythm was pretty technical; now I'm sure.

Introduction

Welcome to the *Groove Essentials* play-along book, the companion to the best-selling *Groove Essentials* DVD. Inside, you'll find everything you need to learn, understand, and execute all 47 grooves demonstrated on the DVD; including truly professional charts, groove variations, helpful hints, and a list of recommended drummers and artists who epitomize each style. The real treasures of this package, however, are the tracks you are going play yourself. There are over 85 original pieces of music (written just for this project) which are the exact tracks I played with on the DVD. With each song more than tripled in length for the disc that accompanies this book, there is more that six hours of music waiting for you to explore. With that much material and variety, guarantee this package will be your musical companion for as long as you play drums.

What is *Groove Essentials*?

Groove Essentials is a groove encyclopedia designed to help any drummer, of any skill level, to become a more complete musician. On the most basic level, it helps students play and understand grooves they didn't know existed, while providing a nice one-stop solution for teachers to explore many groove-related concepts with their students. *Groove Essentials* also gets drummers used to looking at professional sketch charts. (A *chart* is simply musician-slang for a written-out piece of music that a band reads.) These intentionally under-written charts are musical road maps in the style drummers are most likely to see in a professional studio or live session, as opposed to over-notated ink-fests that read more like poorly-translated electronics manuals.

Groove Essentials offers a focused and interactive groove experience for all levels of drummers:

- **BEGINNING** drummers will enjoy playing simple rock beats with a real band, giving them a chance to play the drums with good, solid time, utilizing 4-way coordination.

- **INTERMEDIATE** drummers will have a chance to tackle some syncopated 16th-note grooves and also start playing good swinging jazz.

- **ADVANCED AND PROFESSIONAL** drummers will find 20 challenging world grooves to master, as well as the opportunity to try different feels on jazz shuffles, jazz waltzes, and R&B tunes. The advanced student can also explore changing the tracks' time center by either laying back or pushing ahead intentionally (an entirely different phenomenon than simply dragging or rushing), to create a different feel for the entire song.

Groove Essentials got its start as a collaboration between myself and the Vic Firth Company with the goal of creating a breakthrough groove product for private drumset instructors, schools, and universities. Fifteen drafts and 120 grooves later, the *Groove Essentials* poster was born and became an unprecedented success. Drummers and music educators loved having instant access to a multitude of grooves. Want to talk about a mambo? There it is. To date (2005), there are over 60,000 *Groove Essentials* posters distributed around the globe with over 100,000 anticipated to be in print in a few short years.

After the overwhelmingly positive reaction to the groove posters, it became clear that this information, presented on a DVD with the same obsessive attention to detail and quality, would fill a gaping hole in the world of drumming education: a true, comprehensive DVD groove encyclopedia. So, a little while after the first poster was printed, the *Groove Essentials* DVD, which contained in-depth demonstrations of each groove with music, was created and quickly became a best seller.

As soon as the DVD hit the shelves, my in-box was literally flooded with e-mail from drummers all over the world clamoring to get a copy of the songs I played with on the DVD. I thought that was a great idea, since as an educator myself, I always craved a book I could give students that was a global one-stop solution for learning grooves, reading charts, and playing along with great band tracks. This leads us to where we are now: *Groove Essentials/The Play-Along.*

Funny story—I fondly remember pitching this concept to my friends Rob Wallis and Paul Seigel at Hudson Music long before there was even a finished poster to show them, and I think I was calling it "The Mega-Super-Duper Pack" or something equally eloquent. As usual, they showed their support right away: "No really!" I said excitedly. "It's going to be great . . . three products, all working together to form one interactive system!. . . Wow!" An impossibly long dead silence ensued before Paul mumbled "Hmmm," and Rob said something about how the Yankees need pitching. Anyway, the "Mega-Super-Duper Pack" became *Groove Essentials* (boring!), and now we have an integrated system for *all* levels of drummers who want to learn some new beats from around the corner, and around the world. And, anyway, the Yankees always need pitching.

How This Book Works

Keep in mind that this book works together with the DVD and poster. The book is all about you playing, so there will be blessedly little blabbing on my part. All the information about how to execute and apply the grooves, as well as important conceptual issues, is on the DVD, so I urge you to refer to it if you feel stuck, unsure, or confused. If you think in school terms, it's rather like a take-home test; this book and the included songs are the questions, and the DVD is the source for answers. To help keep things simple, the groove numbers in this book match those on the poster and in the DVD, so it's easy to coordinate what you need.

> **There are six main chapters in *Groove Essentials*:**
>
> 1. **Rock** 2. **Funk** 3. **R&B/Hip-Hop** 4. **Jazz** 5. **World/Specialty.** 6.**Global Tours**

At the beginning of each section, we'll talk briefly about the style we'll be playing; we'll discuss the interesting history and noted players of the style, and other tidbits. We'll also talk about a suggested listening list of artists to get you started on the road to authenticity (please, don't be offended if your personal favorite isn't on the recommended list, it's simply impossible to include everyone). This list can acquaint you with some new music, broaden your musical knowledge, and help you get a grip on each style. (Search the Web to add to your list.) Discover the music and the drummers that people are talking about, and jump in!

Each groove (fig. 1), as well as each tempo, gets its own dedicated page in the book. The groove for the song will be written out at the top of the page (this is the same groove that's on the poster).

Rock Groove 4 FAST

Fig. 1

Next, I'll offer a couple of groove variations for your amusement (fig. 2). The variations are interesting to explore because some of them can stand on their own, and some are just enough to throw in once in awhile. Often, the variations are a bit more technically and rhythmically sophisticated than the original groove. If you're a beginner, you should feel absolutely no pressure to play these grooves if it isn't quite time yet. The grooves will be there for you when your skill level rises. Have patience! As I said on the DVD, "You get zero points for playing hard things badly." Besides, the original grooves are the ones I would play the majority of time and the variations are just that—variations. Feel free to make up your own variations, too.

Groove variations:

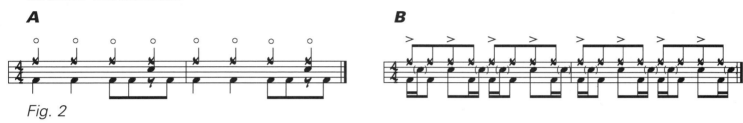

Fig. 2

Next is the chart for the song (fig. 3).

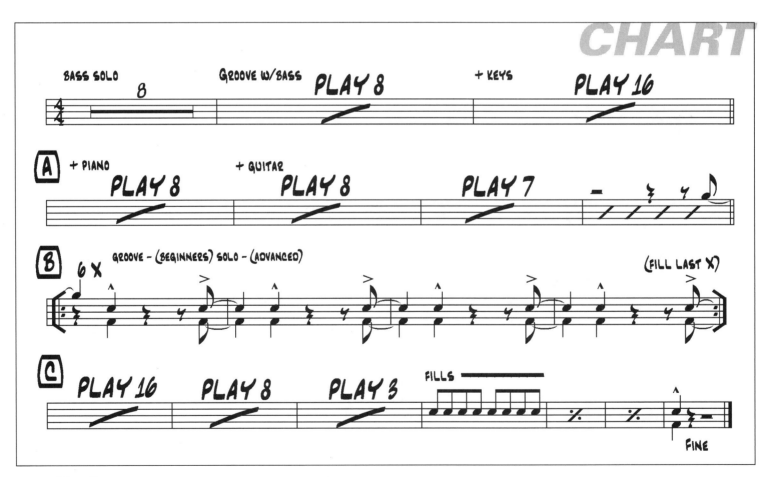

Fig. 3

Below the chart, in the brief discussion section, I'll talk about some points that are pertinent to the groove and song. Song form, chart tips, discussions about the variations, and important points about the tracks are all fair game topics.

What if you don't read music?

The main focus of *Groove Essentials* is on you *playing* the songs, not reading the charts, so don't worry if you can't read music very well or even at all. You can play the songs without reading the charts. However, for those who wish to read the charts (which I hope is all of you!), here's some good news: ninety per cent of reading drum charts is counting bars and knowing where you are in the piece; so if you can feel a beat, you can follow along with the music, even if you can't read very well. I recommend all serious players learn to read music moderately well, but only the most basic reading skills are required to read the charts. If you stumble on a rhythm that you can't figure out, just listen to the music, and use your ears and eyes to gradually make sense of what you see on the page. Just take it slow and follow the charts, even if they are confusing at first; as time goes on, you'll soon see that it all makes sense. Good readers will enjoy seeing the different ways the rhythms are presented in the charts. Of course, if you don't read, a good teacher can help quicken the process, so study privately, if you can. Don't worry if it's confusing on day one. Often, what is confusing today becomes clear tomorrow.

What about fills and solos?

Don't play any . . . just kidding, sort of. While writing this book, I put some of these charts in front of my own students, and without warning, started the CD track to see what they would do. Almost all asked in a panicked tone, "Wait! Is it okay to fill?" I replied, "I guess we'll see, won't we." Though that answer sounds glib, it's the truth. Your fills will decide if it is indeed okay, or

not. Actually, in almost every song there are spots where it's appropriate and necessary to fill; where, if you didn't fill, you'd sound silly. Part of a musical drummer's job is to help introduce new sections of music and set up figures with fills. However, please remember the title of the book: It's not *Play-a-Lotta Notes Essentials!* (Hmmm, I smell a new book!)

All fills for *Groove Essentials* generally serve one of two purposes: to help connect two sections of music together—the end of an $\boxed{A}$ section into the beginning of a $\boxed{B}$ section, for example—or to fill a space in the music. Also, a fill can be as simple as a single,soft, well-placed note on a cymbal bell, or, to another extreme, it can be a furious psycho-like run around the toms. You can hear me do all this and more on the DVD, though hopefully, I try to stay away from the psycho stuff.

As in professional charts, the charts in *Groove Essentials* don't *tell* you to fill every time you should. You are expected to know when and where to fill, because *you* are the drummer. You learn to do all this stuff through trial and error, recording yourself, listening to great drummers and getting feedback from teachers and fellow musicians. I want *Groove Essentials* to be there with you for years and years, and with charts that aren't over-notated, you won't get used to being babied unrealistically. While honing your musical instincts, you can make mistakes and have successes of your design, without the chart telling you what to do every moment.

While fills are often a judgment call, solos are not. The very definition of "solo" means you are all by yourself, so you have to play. However, don't let the word "solo" intimidate you. The spotlight at Madison Square Garden isn't shining on you. In *Groove Essentials*, as in real life, the majority of solos you'll be playing will be to connect sections of music. In fact, many of the solos in the charts could be called fills, depending on who wrote the chart. For example, in the jazz section, you have many 2- and 4-bar solos at the end of the phrase that brings us back around for another chorus of swinging time. Those solos shouldn't be drum features, per se, but rather smooth musical contributions that re-introduce the band for the next chorus. You can just play some swinging time in those solos if you like and then slowly start to expand from there. In short, your drum solos should be just like fills; they should flow and be related to the grooves, not be a separate island of self-gratifying drumming machismo. Solos can sometimes appear in odd places, such as in Groove 47, for example, which starts with a 2-bar drum solo, a very unusual, but musically intriguing twist!

If you're having trouble knowing if your fills are musically appropriate, just remember this little nugget: *Your grooves and fills should sound related to one another.* That simply means that you don't whip haphazardly around the kit at Warp-Factor-9 when playing "Groove 2 Slow." Heck, you may not want to play any fills at all in that song, but if you do, make sure they sound *related* to that particular groove. As always, just refer to the DVD for some examples of simple fills that work and don't get in the way of the song or the groove. Treat each song individually, just like it was a new person you are meeting for the first time. Be polite and courteous, yet confident in yourself. Pieces of music have personalities too, just like people. One piece might need active fills, while another needs practically none at all. Let your ears guide you musically.

Lastly, don't be afraid to try the same song with different goals. Try one pass with almost no fills, and then try another more adventurously, adding several fills, just to see what you create. Try playing in the style of a drummer you admire, striving to guess what he or she might play. All of these techniques can be used to inspire you to new creativity. You are going to play a lot of really bad fills when you practice this way, but that's exactly what is supposed to happen. That's how you learn to tell the good fills from the bad ones, and, as an added bonus; it's totally fun.

About the Charts

"FEATURING PROFESSIONAL CHARTS!" If I had a dime for every time I saw that on a book cover . . . well, as a professional chart reader, I have to tell you that the majority of these charts, as we discussed, are over-notated and quite unprofessional. The charts in *Groove Essentials* are clean and sparse, intentionally under-written, and if you are seeking answers as to what to play where, almost useless. And why are they like that? Because, in a professional situation, it is assumed the drummer *knows* what to play where and when. About the only charts I've seen over-notated in a professional situation are for Broadway musicals; the composers know that, if the musical is a hit, hundreds of musicians from all over the world will be playing their music for decades. However, even that is becoming less common as the musical theatre landscape shifts to more contemporary music.

You see, drum charts aren't supposed to be answer books. They are wide-area maps that tell you the basic stuff about a song, so that you can make smart drumming decisions. That's good, because it gives us the room to be creative and make mistakes in the practice room. Making mistakes is important, because if you don't make mistakes, you don't grow. Sometimes your playing will sound good, sometimes not so good. Take some chances and record yourself. It isn't the easiest path, and it may be painful to listen to on playback, but you'll learn ten times faster than simply playing what you already know over and over. And while we can destroy all the evidence of our horrible fills, I recommend keeping even the worst of your recordings around for awhile. Tuck them away in a box for six months or so and then take a listen. I'll bet you'll be amazed at your progress.

At the bottom of each page, I'll talk briefly about the charts and groove variations, alerting you to any little pitfalls that may be awaiting you. Beginners should read each page first and listen through each song *before* playing, while following the chart and counting along without drumming. You'll soon notice how almost every chart is comprised of 8-bar phrases. This is very intentional, because the vast majority of popular music is built on symmetrical phrases divisible by the number 4. Four, 8, 12, 16, 24, and 32 bars are all standard phrase lengths for popular music styles; therefore, we built the majority of songs for *Groove Essentials* on these common forms.

A SIGHT-READING DRILL FOR ADVANCED PLAYERS:

If you consider yourself an advanced player, you might try the following ear-training exercise that I use in my private teaching:

■ Set yourself up behind your drums with a blank sheet of paper in front of you on your snare drum and have your pencil ready. Your *Groove Essentials* book should be closed.

■ Select "play" for the track you are working on, and in one pass, write a chart and memorize the piece. Remember, only one pass to listen and write your chart simultaneously, and no peeking at my chart.

■ Now, it's your turn. Get yourself ready to play and go for a perfect take with only your chart in front of you. Record yourself and then listen back.

■ Analyze your performance: How did you do? Were you with the band? Did you catch all the figures? Was your time center consistent from beginning to end? Was your phrasing aligned with the band? Were your fills appropriate or self-indulgent? What kind of sound did you get from the drums? Want to try again? Want to fix your chart, perhaps? Try a second take right away if you like. Listen back again.

■ Now compare my chart to yours and see what you missed and what you got right. This is a great drill to prepare you for professional studio work where, sometimes, charts aren't provided, and you might like to quickly sketch a road map for yourself.

HERE ARE A FEW UNIVERSAL CHART EXPLANATIONS:

■ Remember, charts are maps. One of the most common ways to quickly write a bunch of groove bars is the "Play X" method. So, when you see the term "Play 8," that means play 8 bars of groove. When you see "Play 4," play 4 bars of groove. Easy. It's a lot simpler to read (and write) than when every single bar is written out.

■ As on professional charts, you'll see very few dynamics on the charts. Most composers only notate sudden or unusual dynamic shifts on charts, because they expect the drummer to have the expertise to know what volume is necessary for a style or section. Listen to the band. Crunchy, fat guitars need louder drums than a piano trio, right?

■ You will, however, see common-sense notes about instrumentation. "+Gtr.," for example, means that the guitar is added on the next phrase. "Bass out" doesn't mean the bass player was thrown out of the band, but rather, that he is laying out (not playing) on the next section.

■ When we encounter a new chart notation, such as multiple endings, I'll always discuss it at the bottom of the page below the chart and give you clear instructions on how to handle the new direction.

■ The Italian term "fine" you see at the end of the songs means you've come to the end of the piece.

On the DVD, especially on the faster-tempo songs, I take liberties with the beats to give them a little twist, sometimes subtle, sometimes a more obvious skewing. Now it's your turn. Get comfortable with the grooves as written and then, have some fun! Make up your own grooves, too. For now, don't worry about making mistakes. The idea is to have fun, be creative, and go for it. In the future, you'll want to go for perfect takes, and, by all means, knock yourself out. Again, record yourself! You must listen back to truly judge your performance.

About the Songs

Perhaps you heard not long ago about the five musicians who vanished without a trace, then reappeared, looking tired and unshaven—"haggard" is a good word to describe their condition. From their drool-encrusted mouths came strange mutterings, such as, "How many more grooves, Tommy? Please, tell me!" and "36, Nañigo—fast, again? NOOO!" Sadly, these poor souls obviously hadn't slept for days and were in very bad need of a shower.

I confess, I was the kidnapper and while not proud of my actions, it had to be done. I almost felt bad at times for their ordeal . . . almost. Someone whined, "But . . . but . . . I have kids, Tommy!" "Quiet!" I barked, "Or we'll record "Groove 17 Slow" again, and we don't want that, do we?" My prisoners were kept docile with a steady stream of pizza and beer, which, as usual, kept them calm and playing their instruments superbly.

Seriously, all these musicians are (were?) my friends, and I'm really glad they are because otherwise, I could never afford them. My job, other than to organize the project and music at the recordings, was to keep them in the dark for as long as possible about the size of Groove

Essentials. "Just a little project, no big deal," I think were my exact words to lure them into my studio before locking all the doors. When we got to about "Groove 12," the guitarist asked, "Tommy, how many of these are we doing?" "Couple more, almost done," I replied. "Here, have some pizza!" Two days later, shielding their eyes from the brightness of natural light, they were set free. Funny, I haven't seen them since, and I can't understand why they don't return my calls.

All the songs were recorded as a "band," with the musicians playing in the same place, at the same time. That's important to know, because it is the bedrock of the *Groove Essentials* concept:

■ No digitally manipulated parts, which would ruin the group-feel of the band, that we worked so hard to create. What these great musicians played on the original recordings stayed the way they played it.

■ No samples, loops, or pre-made music from any source whatsoever, except on "Groove 15 Slow." This is an example of a modern R&B/Hip-Hop track where loops and samples are as much a part of the genre (for better or worse) as an acoustic bass is in jazz music.

■ The tracks given to you without a click (for beginners, a click track is a metronome clicking sound that runs simultaneously with the music).

To be a drummer who can contribute musically, you must know your role: Rhythmically, you are the sole unifying force for the band. *You are the common thread that all the musicians listen to, to create the groove.* While all the musicians in a band have a responsibility to create grooves, the drums are the foundation upon which most grooves are built. With these tracks played by expert musicians and left in their natural state, drummers of all levels can enjoy the unique interpretation and feel of each piece. Let those factors influence your performance. The options for the drummer to manipulate the track's *feel* are limitless; I'm sure you'll have as much fun as I did finding that perfect groove.

The last point is probably the most important. There is blessedly little click track on these songs. You must groove with the music, without a constant "thwack, thwack" dictating your every move. That, my friends, is a real groove situation. Honestly, on a real gig (unless you are in a studio or playing with a live band that needs timing perfection, for a 30-second jingle or pre-recorded vocals, for example), the entire band listens to you for everything rhythmic. *You* are the metronome. *You* are the click track for the band. From *you*, the band gets:

■ The overall tempo

■ The time center (center, pushing, or laying back)

■ The subdivisions of the sixteenths

■ Where the backbeat lies inside the groove

■ The tightness or looseness of the swing

■ The lilt of the samba (Brazilian)

■ The phrasing of the clave on Afro-Cuban grooves (son or rhumba/2:3 or 3:2)

■ The relentless energy and drive of the merengue

■ All the little intangibles that can't be put into words that make the band groove

The absence of a click does two things:

- First, it makes the music more challenging to play, because all your time problems are magnified without a click controlling your time center. If your time drifts, there is no click to rescue you.

- Second, it forces you to listen to the *music*, not the click. Your *relationship* to the music is your click. All the tracks in *Groove Essentials* are rock-solid and don't move tempo-wise, so you can play with absolute confidence that the tempos aren't fluctuating underneath you. They breathe naturally, *within* the tempo, but the tempo never moves.

That's a problem when practicing only with music that has a click track (or even percussion loops); the student focuses on the click at the expense of the music. Now to be sure, playing with a click is a very important skill; in fact, in today's musical environment, it's essential. Indeed, to get your time sharpened to a fine edge, you must spend exorbitant amounts of time

practicing with metronomes and metronome-like tools. However, with all that time practicing with a click, you must use care that a *dependency* on the click, an all-too-common phenomenon, isn't developed. If you get so used to playing with a click that you can't play confidently without it, then you are *truly useless* as a drummer.

With *Groove Essentials*, you'll have the opportunity to be that organic common thread for a band. You'll have the experience of catching the groove wave, and riding it through the tune. You have to listen to the bass, or piano, or guitar, or percussion, or even better, all of them at the same time. It all depends on the song, since different instruments lead in different songs, but the important thing is, you'll be listening *carefully*.

Two more important facts about the songs: These songs were recorded with a rhythm-section focus; there aren't many solos going on over the top of the groove. In this way, we can focus on what makes a groove really groove. Second, the audio mixes of the songs are made for you to record with. I've left some sonic space for *your* drums. These songs are just begging you to record with them. So, in whatever capacity you have, be it a cheap Walkman® type thing or a spiffy computer-based system, record yourself! (I've said this about ten times already, though I can't emphasize it enough.) Only when listening back to your playing will you truly hear yourself and understand all these concepts we've been discussing.

Now, how do I know this all works? Because on the DVD, I played to every single track this exact same way: playing to each track, no click, just the *music*. That's why I always say to refer to the DVD if you have any problems lining up your part with the tracks and want to hear what everything is supposed to sound like. I'm playing with *exactly* what you are hearing on your CD. The only difference is that each track is around three times its original length so that you can sit in each groove for a really long time. I've also changed some arrangements to make them more challenging for intermediate and advanced players.

The global tours toward the end of this book are 15-minute extravaganzas that use five different grooves combined in one piece. I used to make my own practice mixes on cassette (wow, remember those?) when I was a kid—Buddy Rich into Stevie Wonder into Meatloaf into Paquito D'Rivera—and here I did it for you. If you aspire to play professionally, you'll need to be able to shift grooves on the fly. That's what the global tours are all about. Have fun with them. Oh, one more thing; all the tracks feature a 2-bar count-off unless otherwise announced at the beginning of the track.

We're all in this together, and I'm absolutely positive you'll have a great, great time! Watching my own private students play with these tracks has been a revelation for me and for them. They may not play a track perfectly the first time, but each subsequent time gets better, and they really listen and react to the music. So will you.

Enough already! Let's get into it. Now, in the privacy of your practice room, you can experiment with many styles and tracks that already have an organic flow, and you can find that common thread that binds the band together. Let's get to work . . .

If things get rough, remember my favorite piece of advice:
Music isn't a race! Take your time and enjoy the journey, mistakes and all.

Tommy Igoe

Chapter 1
ROCK Grooves

In 1951, "rock 'n' roll" was given its name by Cleveland disc jockey Alan Freed; things have never been the same since. Though most associate it with loud drums, backbeats, and electric guitar, rock 'n' roll is deeply rooted in rhythm and blues, and its first artists can be directly linked to the R&B tradition. Over the years, the music has changed, and continues to change drastically, but one of the hallmarks of rock 'n' roll has always been a deep commitment to the "beat." Even in the earliest recordings, you can hear the relentless drive of the rhythm section, which is the genre's calling card.

There are three types of rock grooves we'll be discovering together in *Groove Essentials*, and they are the foundation for any direction you want to go. I'll bet some students using this book fantasize about playing in the biggest arenas with the craziest bands, while others want to join a group playing all 1960s classic rock just for kicks. Perhaps some of you are jazzers who have a weak backbeat and no concept of manipulating your time center in straight eighth-note music. Regardless of your own personal desires, we have a common goal: to sound as good as we possibly can.

THE THREE DIFFERENT ROCK GROOVES IN CHAPTER 1 ARE:

■ **Eighth-note grooves**   ■ **Sixteenth-note grooves**   ■ **Half-time grooves**

Each section has its own signature feel that is clearly illustrated with each song.

Here are some drummers, listed in no particular order, to look for when thinking about rock. They cross all generations and styles; some are young, some are old, some play busy, some play sparse, some hit hard, others barely at all; it doesn't matter. What matters is that they are all great players playing their interpretation of rock. Have a listen and see what inspires you.

Kenny Aronoff *(John Mellencamp and others)*	Joey Kramer *(Aerosmith)*
Carter Beauford *(Dave Matthews Band)*	Mitch Mitchell *(Jimi Hendrix)*
Cindy Blackman *(Lenny Kravitz)*	Keith Moon *(The Who)*
John Bonham *(Led Zeppelin)*	Neil Peart *(Rush)*
Vinnie Colaiuta *(Sting, Frank Zappa)*	Jeff Porcaro *(Toto)*
Phil Collins *(Genesis)*	Chad Smith *(Red Hot Chili Peppers)*
Stewart Copeland *(The Police)*	Ringo Starr *(The Beatles)*
Taylor Hawkins *(Foo Fighters)*	Charlie Watts *(Rolling Stones)*
Jim Keltner *(Legendary studio drummer)*	Alex Van Halen *(Van Halen)*

choose one for the 9th March 2013

ROCK

Grooves 1- 5 can be played on the Hi-Hat or Ride Cymbal

Variation A   **Variation B**

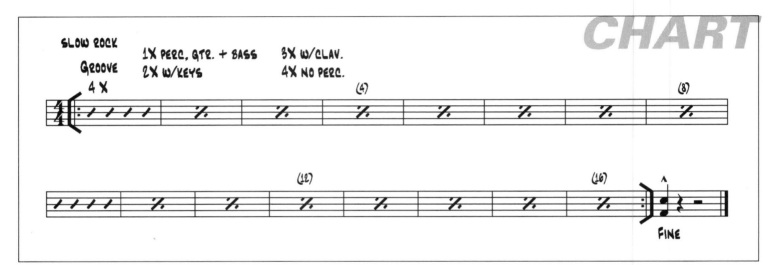

Alright then, off we go with a no-frills slinky rock tune that uses a very simple groove and chart. One glance at the chart and you can easily see this is a 16-bar song form and we're going to repeat that form four times. Take a look at the instrumentation description at the beginning. This description clues you in on what instruments are playing each time through:

■ **The first time, you are playing with guitar, percussion, and bass.**

■ **The second time through, keyboards are added.**

■ **The third time, the clavinet enters.**

■ **And the last time, the percussion drops out.**

Read these descriptions carefully for all the charts. They will help you make smart musical choices for groove variations and dynamics.

When the percussion drops out the last time through, you may feel as if your friend, who you were so nicely locking up with, suddenly abandoned you. Repeat after me: "Thou shall not drift when the percussion stops." No, when the percussion stops, you must dig in to the time even *deeper*. Drive that bus, baby.

The groove variations are very subtle additions to the basic groove, with "subtle" being the key word. If you play them loud and silly you'll just sound, well, loud and silly. If you don't like the variations or how you are playing them, set them aside for another day. This basic groove is such an important groove, and the mother of so many other grooves, that it's really all you need for this song and many others. It's technically the easiest groove in this book, but one of the hardest to play really well.

ROCK
Groove 1 FAST Track 02

Variation A   **Variation B**

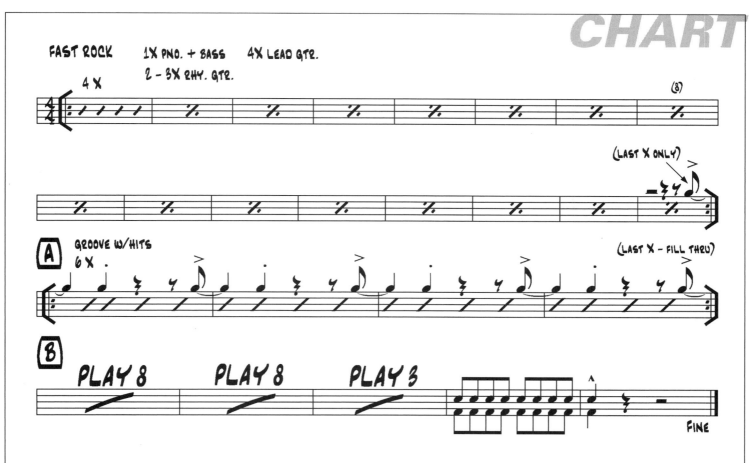

Now let's play the same groove at a faster tempo. The flavor of this and every other groove feels different in your hands and ears at a brighter tempo and, as a result, you'll encounter different things happening (good and bad) to yourself and the other musicians.

This track features the piano out front playing a 4-bar riff as the main theme of the track, like a Billy Joel/Elton John vibe. The brightness of the piano is great, because it gives us something to hang onto when the guitars kick in. Thankfully, the bass plays a simple connective line and refuses to get pulled into the mischief of the other musicians. The solidity of the bass gives you some options: Variation A is more active and Variation B has an intentional rhythmic rub where it intentionally doesn't line up with the bass part. Make up a few grooves of your own, and ask yourself *the* question: "Is this groove serving the song?"

On the chart, Letter A has a great ensemble riff that you groove through. Inflect the ensemble riff in your groove; if you aren't sure what to do, play the basic groove with no changes. Check out the DVD and copy what I did, then try it yourself.

ROCK

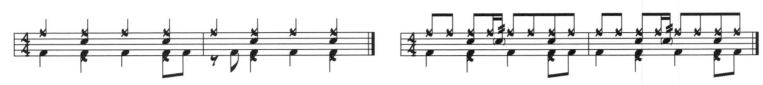

Variation A   **Variation B**

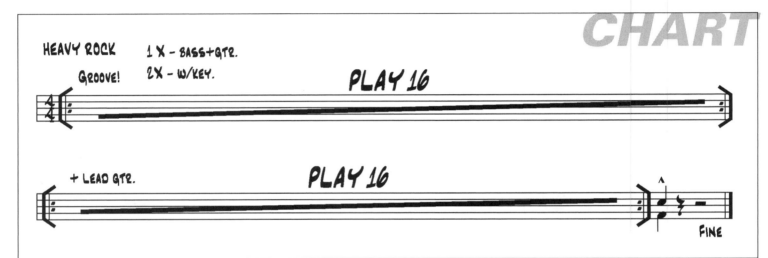

CHART

"Four-on-the-floor" is the ultimate bar-band groove, and this song is the ultimate bar-band riff. If you've done any quickie bar-band gigs, you'll know exactly what I mean when you hear it. The guitarist says "G!" and off he goes with the rest of us in tow. I love this song; it's so simple and undeniably heavy. It's fat and dense and, well, I think I've made the point that this song needs to go on a diet. Am I coming through out there? Dig in on this big groove.

First things first—don't flam! This is an extremely layered groove, where parts are playing together, as opposed to a linear groove, where they are playing separately. If the parts don't line up *perfectly* (in the drum world, we call that misalignment "flamming"), this groove is over before it starts. So, practice alone for awhile just playing the groove with a metronome, and listen to the quality of sound coming from your drumset. That's good advice for *all* the grooves, actually.

Variations, eh, who needs them? This groove is perfect. But we're not robots, so throwing a little spice in now and then is a good thing. Variation A avoids "1" every other bar, which is a good way to slightly lighten the load, if desired. Variation B is one of my favorites; those gooshy little buzzes on the snare are a unique sound that lets everyone know there's a real drummer back there.

ROCK
Groove 2 FAST Track 04

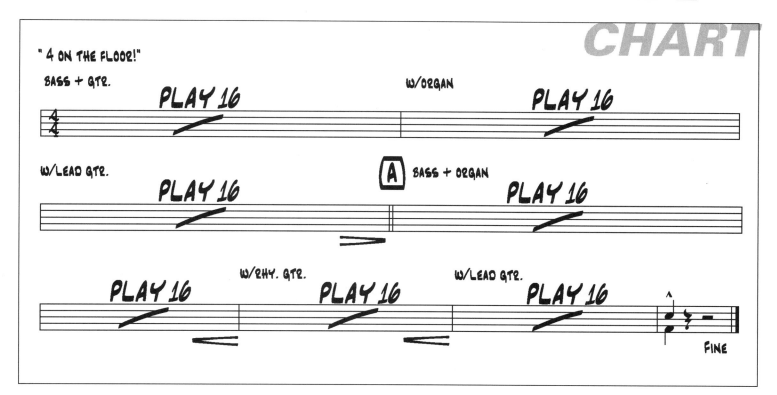

Variation A

Variation B

"Four-on-the-floor" is another animal entirely when played at a faster tempo. The human tendency to become sloppy and create "flamming parts" is magnified by, oh, I don't know, about a million times at this tempo. Don't ask me why; I have no idea. It's just one of those facts we take for granted: The sky is blue, the grass is green, and "four-on-the-floor" turns to flamming slop at faster tempos if you aren't careful.

The chart is telling us that we're again playing 16-bar phrases with different instruments coming in and out. Letter A decreases in intensity, so you can really focus on the groove, as you play with just the organ (possibly the coolest instrument ever, except the drums, of course) and bass for a lengthy 32 bars. Then we build with more and more guitar, so naturally, you would build right along with the track. Don't lower your intensity just because you decrease your volume. No, no, no—your intensity should remain high no matter what volume you play.

The variations give you something to toy with at this tempo. Especially Variation B provides a different twist: The right hand eighth notes are played on the floor tom instead of the hi-hat. Talk about a completely different sound—use it wisely and don't hurt anybody.

ROCK

Groove 3 SLOW Track 05

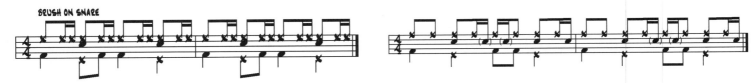

(ONLY WHEN PLAYING RIDE)

Variation A   **Variation B**

BRUSH ON SNARE

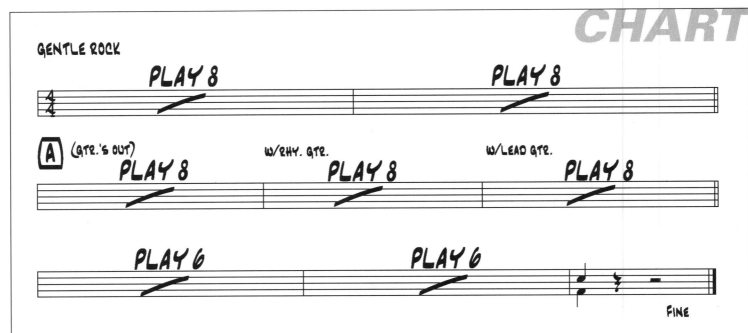

CHART

GENTLE ROCK

A (GTR.'S OUT)   W/RHY. GTR.   W/LEAD GTR.

PLAY 8   PLAY 8   PLAY 8   PLAY 8   PLAY 8

PLAY 6   PLAY 6

FINE

I don't know how a bunch of jaded musicians like us made a track so warm and fuzzy, but here it is. We called this song "French Roast" because it sounds as if it would make a nice coffee jingle. Groove-wise, this one is another got-to-know, because it works so many times on so many songs. It's easy to play; I find that students get a handle on this bass drum pattern with less flamming than on the previous two grooves.

It's easy to see from the chart that we're playing 8-bar phrases now—close cousins to the 16-bar phrase. When the guitars drop out at Letter A, focus carefully on your time consistency, because if you drift, this is where it will be. There is a glorious amount of space that needs to be connected; your groove is that *connective tissue*. On the DVD, you find me talking a lot about the connective tissue of grooves and conceptualizing what binds grooves together. It's easy to see how the eighth notes in a song like this, where there is so much space, bridge all the gaps and make the song flow forward.

Variation A is one of the best sounds to use in studios on softer grooves where you play the ride pattern with a brush on the snare drum. The left hand can play the backbeat as a cross-stick, or try two brushes on the snare. In the studio, music producers love brushes on the snare instead of the usual hi-hat sound. Variation B has some bass drum/snare drum interplay. Again, dynamics determine if this interplay is a good or bad thing. Play too loud, and this variation sounds like a technical coordination exercise—an effect you definitely want to avoid.

ROCK

Groove 3 FAST Track 06

(ONLY WHEN PLAYING RIDE)

Variation A

Variation B

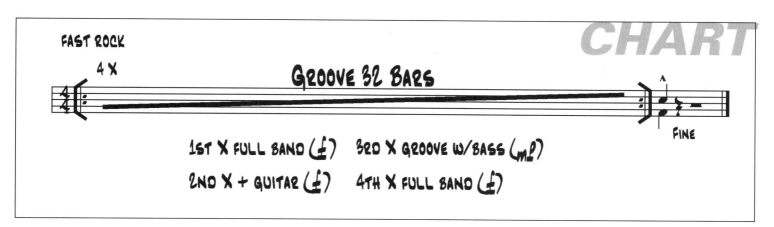

Nice chart, right? When I get a chart like this in a session, I don't know whether to thank the writer or ask, "Are you kidding???" Actually, a chart like this, if you even get one, is really all you need. Obviously, the form is 32 bars and it is repeated four times. This chart, unlike the majority of charts in this book and in real life, has dynamic markings. We're given instrumentation and small dynamics in parentheses. For those of you who are new to dynamics, here's a quick run-down of the Italian on today's menu:

- **PIANISSIMO (abbr. pp): Very soft**
- **PIANO (abbr. p): Soft**
- **MEZZO PIANO (abbr. mp): Medium soft**

- **MEZZO FORTE (abbr. mf): Moderately loud**
- **FORTE (abbr. f): Loud**
- **FORTISSIMO (abbr. ff): Very loud**

Actually, you can see as many as five p's *(ppppp)* or f's *(fffff)*, but in my experience, that's reserved for classical pieces where the composers sometimes like to see how many letters they can squeeze on a page. For the 99.99% of drumset charts that even provide dynamics, the six levels you see above will be all you need to know. Anyway, I'm sure you're all smart enough to figure out that more f's mean to play louder.

The song itself is actually four 8-bar phrases strung together to make one super-sized 32-bar form that is built on the classic two-chord gospel harmony used in thousands of songs. Break it way down the third time through and dig in with the bass. Perhaps a cross-stick instead of the snare would make a nice choice for the backbeat—give it a try, then bring the volume back up for a final gallop through the form.

Variation A is syncopated and flows over the bar line to create a true 2-bar phrase. Variation B is another 2-bar phrase with a lot of interplay between the snare and bass drum. I recommend using both variations as a spice to season the original groove, rather than using either one through the whole song. Needless to say (though I'm going to say it over and over again), your time should be rock solid, regardless of which groove you choose to play.

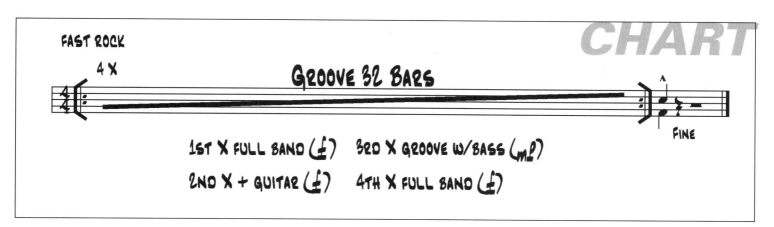

Groove 4 SLOW Track 07

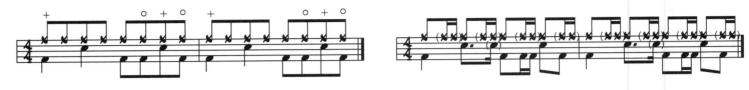

Variation A　　　　　　　　　　　　　　**Variation B**

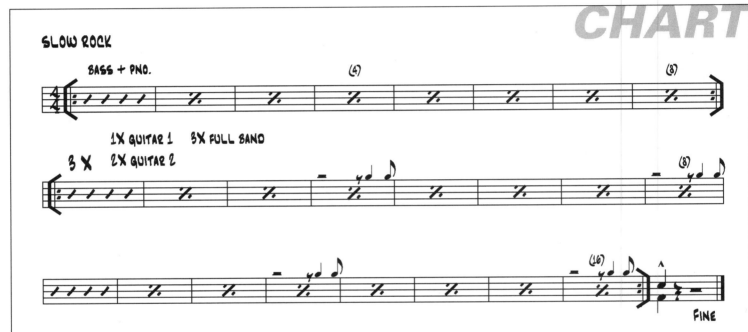

CHART

SLOW ROCK

Compared to the other pieces we've played so far, this song has a completely different feel, because the piano is playing all the eighth notes with you. *Sacrilège! Has he lost his mind? Those are our eighth notes and we shall not part with them.* Now, now, they belong to everyone, so share nicely. Actually, it's a scary thing when too many musicians join in on the subdivisions of beats unless they play with excellent time. Of course, if they have good time, unison rhythms are powerful like nothing else. Lucky for us, our pianist plays with great time, so we can join him on the hi-hat to create a silky smooth undercurrent for this song. There is also a little rhythmic lick that happens every four bars that you can inflect into your groove. Don't *stop* the groove and play a rhythm, just imply that it's there. You can see it notated in the chart, too.

The song itself is a simple 16-bar form that we play four times with different guitars coming in and out, until everybody joins in the last time through. Variation A has an extra note in the bass drum; experience how much weight one note can add to the groove. Variation B is much busier with the classic "chug-chugga-chug" hi-hat rhythm and quite talkative snare and bass drum pattern. Both are very useful variations. Feel free, of course, to make up your own grooves.

Groove 4 FAST Track 08

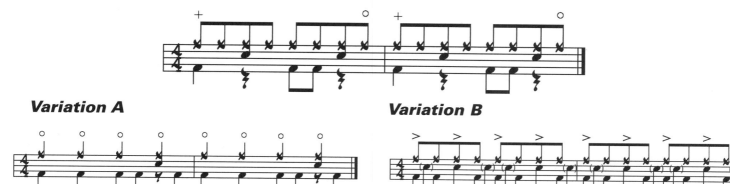

Variation A

Variation B

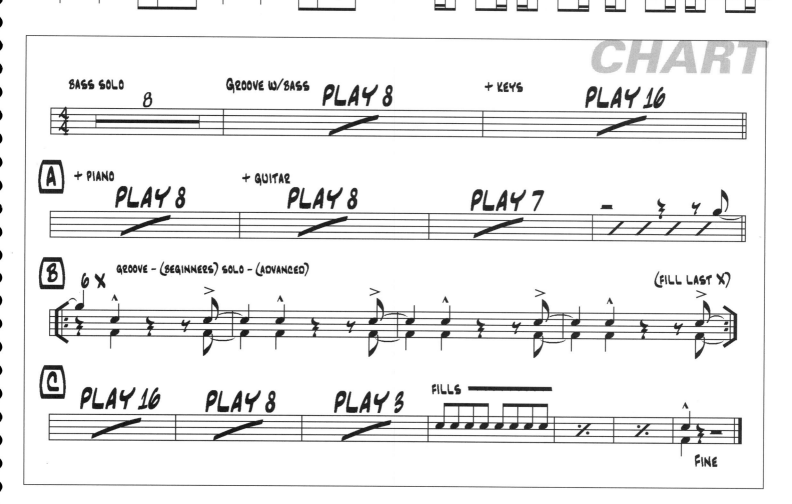

We're using the same chord progression from "Rock Groove 1 Fast," but with an entirely different bass line to illustrate what a powerful tool shifting the groove is. The bass has a solo for 8 bars and then we *join in* with our groove. As drummers, we are used to starting songs; however, when another musicians starts, it can't feel as if the wheels fell off the bus when we join them. Your goal should be solidity from the very first note, without fishing for the time or groove.

There a nice ensemble riff at Letter B that advanced players can solo over while beginners and intermediates can groove through it. On the DVD, I groove through it; the soloing should only be attempted after you have a solid handle on the rhythms. Now that I've appropriately wagged my finger at you, let me say that the riff is great to solo over, so if you have an adventurous soul, knock yourself out.

Variation A is built on a sloshy quarter-note hi-hat playing only the downbeats. This is a great sound that many blues drummers have used for, give or take, a hundred years. Variation B is another classic busy snare drum/bass drum groove. Throw it in once in awhile and it sounds cool and slick; use it too many times and it sounds like a hyperactive drum machine.

Groove 5 SLOW Track 09

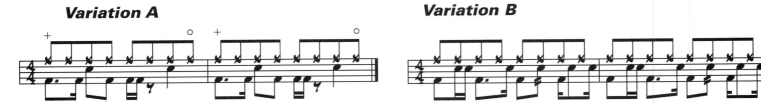

Variation A   **Variation B**

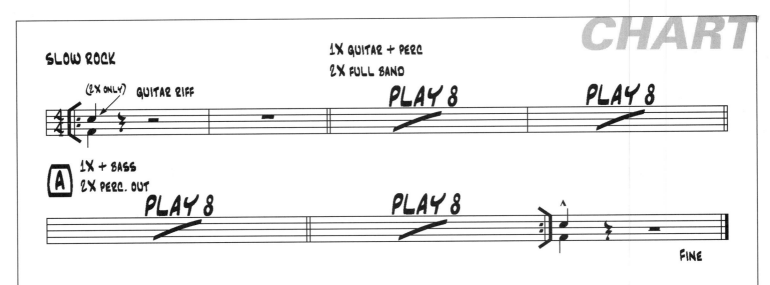

This is a great track to discuss an important matter in greater detail: your *time center*. The concept of a moveable time center refers to *where* you place the groove in relation to the common pulse of the song. Your time center can be in front of (pushing ahead) or behind the beat (laying back), or it can be dead center. For example, since the band is so tight on this track, try seeing what it feels like to play your groove just a little back in relation to the bass line. An excellent way to develop this skill is to play only your hi-hat with the track. Try a pass with fatter heavier eighth notes that sit back a little in relation to the bass line. Perhaps play with the shank of the stick on the hi-hat, rather than the tip, to get a heavier sound and convey the feeling of weight. Then, using the tip of the stick, try a pass with some lighter eighth notes that are leading the band along. *Important: This should not be confused with rushing and dragging.* Rushing is gaining speed, increasing the tempo, while dragging is slowing down the tempo. We never, ever want to rush or drag, unless we are intentionally doing so for musical reasons. Practicing rhythms with a metronome, while keeping these concepts in mind, is essential in order to garner this advanced and very valuable skill.

The song starts with a two-bar guitar riff that is the basis for the feel of the piece. It's just guitar and percussion playing a tight groove, so keep your part tight too. The term "tight" in these situations does not imply playing with tension, but rather playing crisp rhythms with the band. Sloppy playing is often called loose, while precise playing is tight. Your goal should be to play tight right from the first note.

Variation A is a bit funkier than the main groove and works very well with this track. Variation B is a completely new offering: a groove with no obvious backbeat (beats 2 & 4 on the snare). You hear truly funky artists, like Prince, use this technique all the time. They are so confident in their groove that sometimes they don't want a backbeat. You also hear avoidance of backbeats in Caribbean-based dance styles, like reggaeton. Like most drummers, you'll want to reach for your trusty backbeat, so this variation may feel strange when you first play it. Give it a try and see how it works for you. Conceptually, it's a completely different kind of groove, so give it the special treatment it deserves.

Groove 5 FAST Track 10

Variation A

Variation B

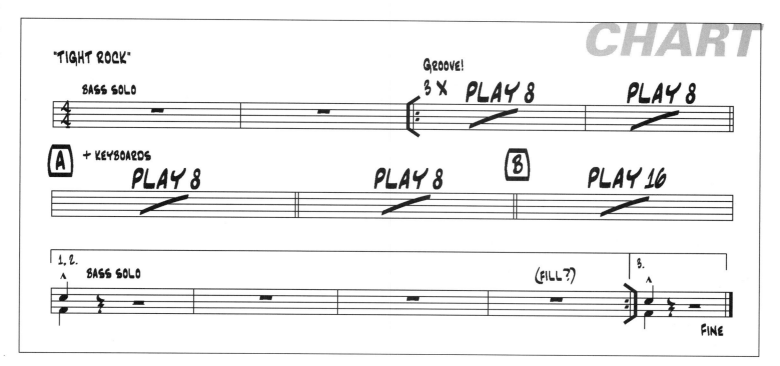

Since everyone in the band loves Steely Dan (Ted Baker, our keyboardist, is currently in Steely Dan), we couldn't resist paying homage to one of the greatest groove bands of all time. True to the "Dan" lineage, this groove is ridiculously tight. "Tight" means crisp and sharp, not tense. You can hear how the band is deeply entrenched in the groove and committed to the time. Often, you can easily hear the musicians intentionally pushing ahead or laying back. Here, however, everyone is phrasing their rhythms exactly the same way: right down the center. You feel this commitment when you listen to the track and sense how effortlessly it propels along; you must bring that same commitment when *you* play without the track, or it will never feel right. Remember, don't hunt for the time! Commit to the groove and don't waver—be solid as a rock.

This chart introduces a new direction, one that is very common: multiple endings. For those unfamiliar with multiple endings, look at the chart now; you can clearly see two phrase endings, one labeled "1,2." and the other labeled "3." We play the form of this chart three times: The first two times we take the ending labeled "1,2." (called "first and second endings"); the third time, we skip over the "1,2." ending and play the ending labeled "3" (the "third" ending). It's that simple. See, I told you this reading thing is easy.

Variation A is deceptive in its simplicity. If you play it sterile, it sounds like a hippie-surfer beat; give it some panache, and it sounds retro-cool. All the notation markings in the world won't help, so experiment and enjoy. Variation B has a hi-hat part that implies a half-time feeling, while the bass and snare drum stay consistent. This is, personally, one of my favorite tracks in the book.

ROCK

Groove 6 SLOW Track 11

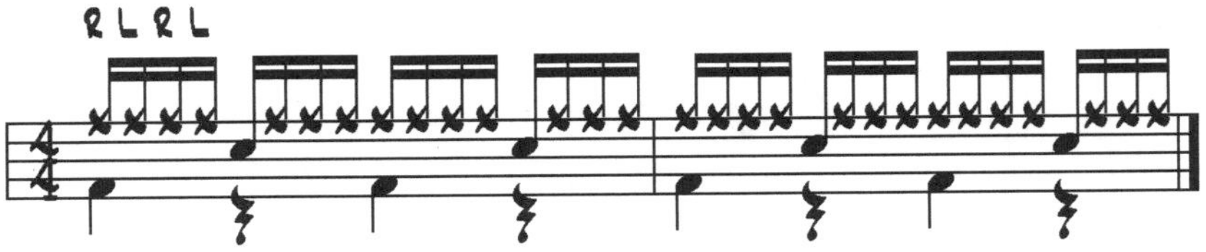
R L R L

Variation A

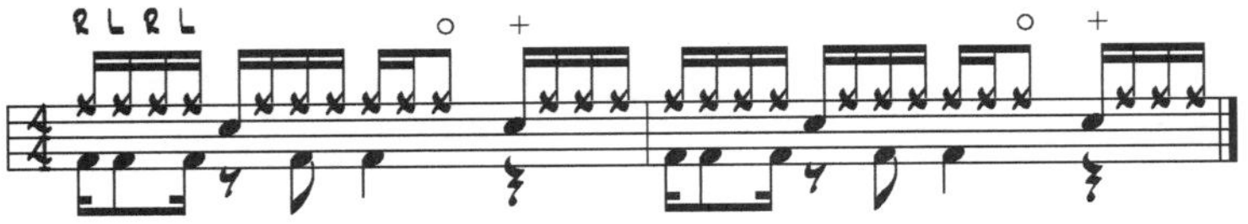
R L R L

Variation B

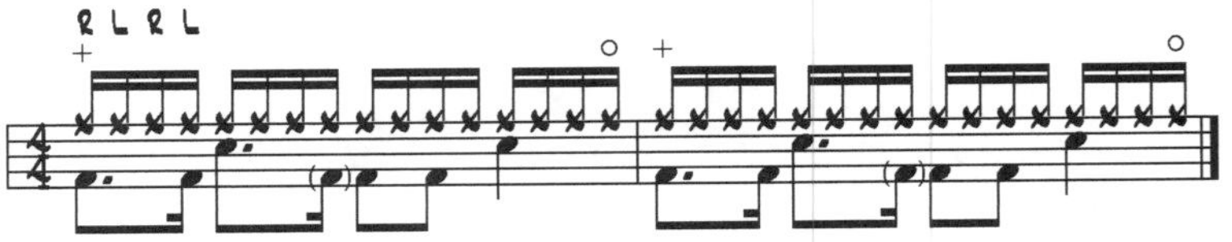
R L R L

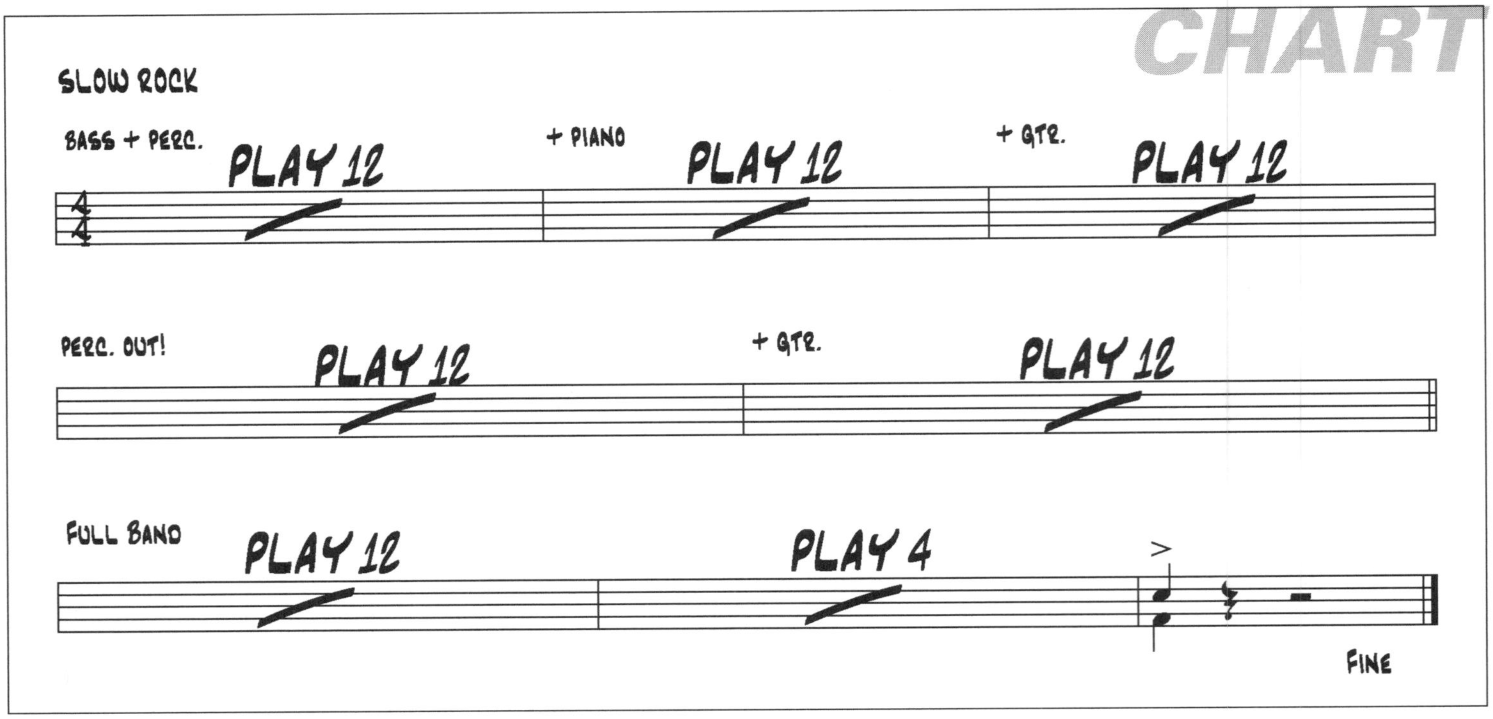
CHART
SLOW ROCK
BASS + PERC.
PLAY 12
+ PIANO
PLAY 12
+ GTR.
PLAY 12
PERC. OUT!
PLAY 12
+ GTR.
PLAY 12
FULL BAND
PLAY 12
PLAY 4
FINE

Groove 6 introduces the first of three sixteenth-note based rock grooves. These two-handed rock grooves should *feel* completely different from the upcoming R&B grooves which are played with one hand. A *two*-handed hi-hat part gives you:

- **More air in your playing**
- **Much more weight on the hi-hat, if desired**
- **Very fast, perfectly even (hopefully!) hi-hat parts, if desired**
- **The ability to get a louder rimshot on the snare because of clean stick logistics with no crossed hands**

Once you explore the feeling of one- and two-handed playing, you'll be able to make the best choice for the music. It's very personal; once you get a handle on it, let the music guide you on what is the right groove.

Variation A has a busier bass drum part, and Variation B has a simpler bass drum part but with a quick open/closed hi-hat motion that can be messy the first time you play it. *The trick with any* open *hat sound is to* close *it within the groove!* Don't close your hi-hats any old place. Listen on playback (you *are* recording, right?); you'll hear what I mean, because hi-hats that close outside the groove are groove-killers.

Take a good look at the chart. Hmmm . . . I don't know, call me old-fashioned, but I'd say we're playing in 12-bar phrases. As always, when the instruments start and stop, *you* are the common link weaving your way through the groove. So, weave away, and make something nice.

ROCK
Groove 6 FAST Track 12

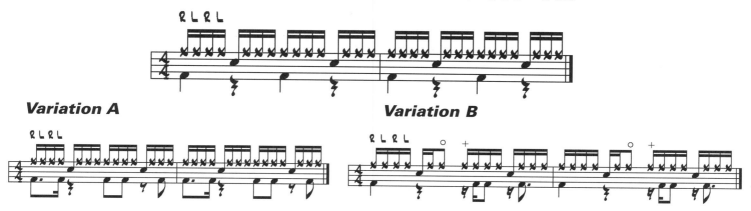

Variation A　　　　　　　　　　　　　**Variation B**

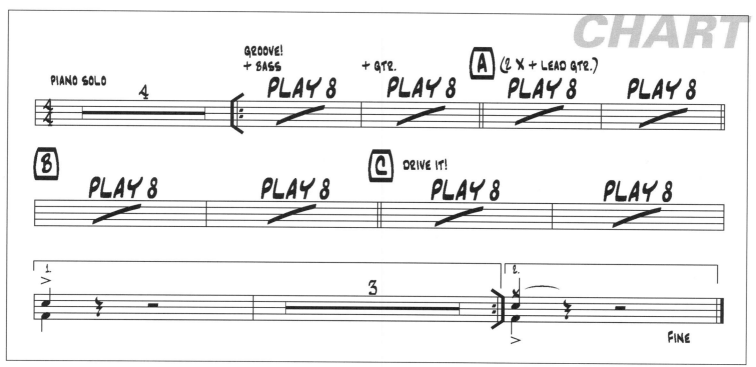

Billy Joel decided to come by the studio and play a track for us! Well, not really, but it sure sounds like he did. Anyway, there is a whole lot of two-handed madness coming from the piano on this track, so that means there is going to be a whole lot of sixteenth notes flying around. That's okay, but man, you have to be committed to the groove, and make this baby line up. When you listen to the track alone, you can hear how it's very solid and well played, but there is something missing. That, my friends, is you! This song really, really *needs* drums to tie it together. It's nice to be needed, isn't it?

Variation A is a great groove you'll love to play. It has a relentless forward drive that works great with this track. Variation B is another great groove that works perfectly with this track, but it's a bit more dangerous. Faster bass drum notes combine with an open hi-hat part to make a groove that either cooks or gets cooked. This would be a great time to once again remind everyone that this isn't a race. Variation B will be here for you tomorrow, I promise.

This chart is straight-ahead. (I got the saying "straight-ahead" from my father, who used it all the time, along with other musicians of his era. It means "no surprises, nothing fancy." I like it, so I'll use it too.) We have the ubiquitous first and second endings on this chart, but you guys are old pros at that now from your experience with "Groove 5-Fast." You can see Letter C needs a little push, so inflect a rise of intensity in your groove. Have fun with this one; it's a great chart.

ROCK
Groove 7 SLOW Track 13

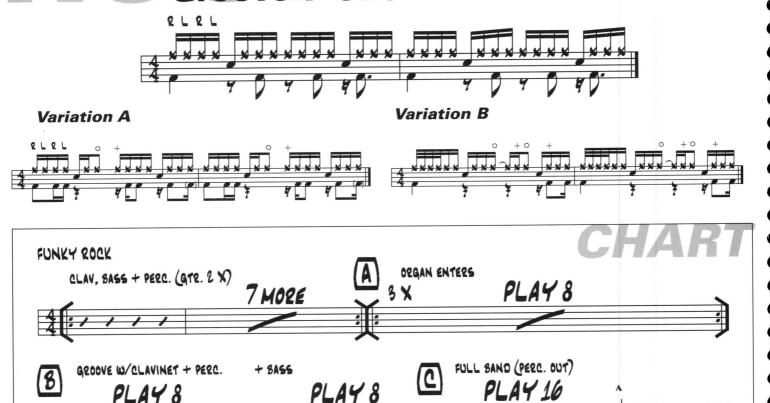

Variation A

Variation B

FUNKY ROCK

CLAV, BASS + PERC. (GTR. 2 X)   7 MORE   [A] ORGAN ENTERS 3 X   PLAY 8

[B] GROOVE W/CLAVINET + PERC.   + BASS   PLAY 8   [C] FULL BAND (PERC. OUT)   PLAY 16

PLAY 8

FINE

This song is so nasty that it could easily be in the funk section too, which again illustrates the powerful influence that we have as drummers on the global flavor of a song. After you play this song down a few times with the grooves on this page, try grabbing a couple of the funk grooves that are introduced in the next chapter, and see how *those* grooves feel with this song. You can try mixing and matching different grooves from different chapters to experiment with what fits and what doesn't. Remember, it's okay to make mistakes right now; we're practicing! I know a few professional chefs, and they all say they had to ruin many soufflés before becoming masters of their art. A little less sugar here and a little more butter there create something new.

Variation A is a great pattern that I think you'll enjoy playing. It's busy without being too thick-sounding; give it a try, and you'll see what I mean. Variation B . . . holy cow, what the heck is that? It looks a little intimidating at first, but it isn't as scary as it seems. It is an advanced groove to be sure, and unless you have some decent coordination and hand technique, this might be a good one to skip for now. However, if you feel up for it, try it as a complement to the main groove of the song. Again, it's a great spice to throw in once in awhile, and if you lay it in the groove just right, it makes people say "Ooooh, I like that!"

This chart is very clear and easy to follow. Take a close look at the first bars of the piece. For beginners, that first bar with the four slash marks is shorthand telling you to groove in the style of the music. It's immediately followed by a "7 More" bar, which, of course, means to play seven more bars. So, there are total of—drum roll, please—eight bars. Our friend, the 8-bar phrase, is back, so please don't think of this chart as a 1+7=8 formula; it's just an 8-bar phrase that happens to look strange on paper. It's much more musically savvy to think of this phrase simply as an 8-bar phrase, and count it that way. The musicians, most of whom are playing melodic instruments, will be thinking "8" as well, definitely not "1+7." Lastly, when the percussion drops out, you are on your own, by yourself, to hold this baby together, so *hold it together*.

ROCK

Groove 7 FAST Track 14

Variation A

Variation B

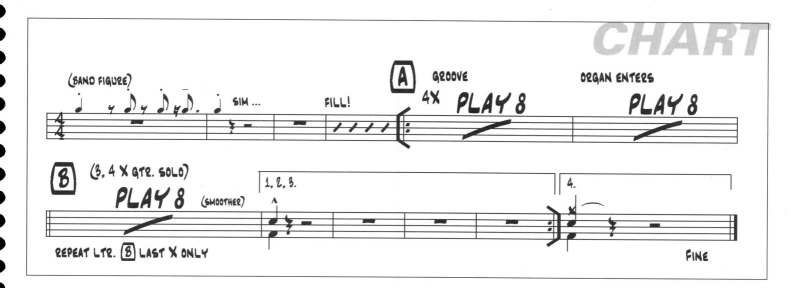

Let's start by talking about the chart. There's a band riff that this entire song is based on; you can see the rhythm in the first two bars of the piece, then we jump in at Letter A with a tight groove. The fast sixteenths cause problems for many drummers of all skill levels. But, have no fear, because I'm going to give you the three secrets to play fast hi-hat grooves like a pro. Pay attention because this is complicated stuff:

1. **Don't play the hi-hat too loud.**
2. **Don't play the hi-hat too loud.**
3. **Don't play the hi-hat too loud!**

Am I coming through out there? Good! The hi-hat is a very powerful instrument, musically speaking, on your drumset. It's definitely the most versatile, and it contributes a unique sound like no other instrument. That power has to be respected and used wisely. Hi-hats are like Tabasco®; a little goes a long way. Watch great hi-hat masters like Buddy Rich or Max Roach. It looks as if they are *dancing* with the hi-hat, not beating it into submission. And while those drummers are jazz drummers, and we are discussing rock grooves; great artistry on the drums transcends genre. Is there a time and place to just recklessly bash the hi-hat? You bet, but this isn't one of them.

We see the word "smoother" at Letter B, so the first thing I would do is simplify the bass drum pattern; Variation B is excellent for that. I play this variation on the DVD, and it has a lot of motion happening on the top part of the drumset, while the bass drum stays simple. Variation A is a hybrid groove of sorts, because it sports a busy first bar and a simple second bar. I love grooves like this because of the natural tension and release both bars convey. Oh, and enjoy the percussion part the *first* two times through the song, because it drops out and leaves you all by yourself to mind the store the *last* two times. Must be union . . .

ROCK

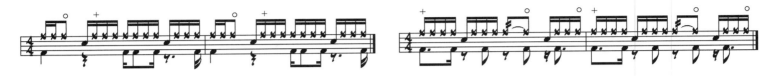

Variation A   **Variation B**

I don't know why, but after watching students, I can tell you the tendency will be to play this track very deliberately and hard, but when you listen to the music, does it sound "hard" to you? No, of course not—it sounds like it's a cool laid-back vibe, like a lazy Sunday afternoon. With your drums, create that same feeling of "what's the hurry?" Perhaps even sit back on your drum throne a little bit to get that laid-back feeling in your body before you play. Also, the guitar has a non-stop running line throughout the song, so listen closely to your relationship with that part.

I guess the composer was running out of paper when he gave us this chart, because it's only one line and only tells us the most basic of things, like when to stop and start. Welcome to the world of professional charts. However, this chart has a new element to discuss: a repeat within a repeat. It's very simple: The first "Play 4" is repeated to create an 8-bar phrase, and you also repeat the *entire form* four times, so every time you see that "Play 4," repeat it. You might ask yourself, "Why didn't he just write "Play 8"? Actually, there could be many answers to that, such as it's a 4-bar phrase repeated twice, and he wanted to visually depict that. Or, on the other hand, maybe he accidentally wrote "Play 4" and didn't feel like erasing it, so he just put repeats around it. Who knows? Who cares? It's an 8-bar phrase.

Variation A has a bass drum part that deliberately goes against the bass line to create some tension. Rhythmic tension is a phenomenal tool to use in grooves and creates suspense for the listener until the point when you decide to resolve the tension by lining things up again. So, perhaps, to create some musical friction, you might like to drop in some tension ever so often, while relying on the main groove as your base. Variation B has tension and release all in the same groove! The first half of each bar aligns with the bass line, while the second half rubs against it. And, for extra added value, it also has a very cool roll, making it even slicker. Is the roll causing a problem for you? Simple—don't play it; just groove through it and add it later.

ROCK

Groove 8 FAST Track 16

Variation A

Variation B

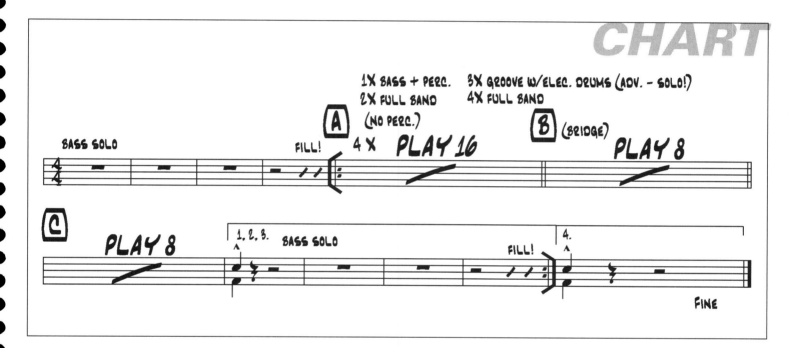

Besides being fun to play, this song is a real workout; that's one of the reasons I like playing it so much. When I'm finished, I like feeling that I did something physical, and this tune does it for me big-time. Lots to discuss here, so let's get into it . . .

The chart is straight-ahead with no surprises. The first time through, the drums groove with the bass and percussion. Listen closely to the music; this is a great opportunity to hear two different time centers happening simultaneously. The percussion, predictably, is spot on, and very forward in the groove. The bass is just a touch fatter—not late, not dragging—just fatter. So, what are you going to do about it? There is no click (*you* are the click, remember?), so it's all up to you. There is a time center right in the middle of the percussion and the bass and, when you find it, it will be as if you just bit into your favorite dessert—perfect!

The keyboard and guitar come in the second time through with the guitar playing a busy strum part that lines up nicely with your groove. The third time through has an interesting twist: electronic drums. Playing with pre-programmed drum parts is very common nowadays, and the reasons you may have to do so are numerous. So, if you want to just groove, then groove. *If you want to solo over the drums, then take a solo. If you decide to groove, you absolutely must lock dead-on with the electronic drums.* This is a time when all your practice with a click will pay off. No flams, no excuses. Just do it. The last time through the form is just you and the band.

Both Variations A and B have more interplay than the main groove. Variation B in particular is quite busy. Is it too busy? Yes, if you play it badly and obnoxiously. Not at all if you are sensitive and musical, and exercise restraint. Hey, it's been over 30 seconds since I've asked if you are recording yourself. Are you?

ROCK

Groove 9 SLOW Track 17

Variation A

Variation B

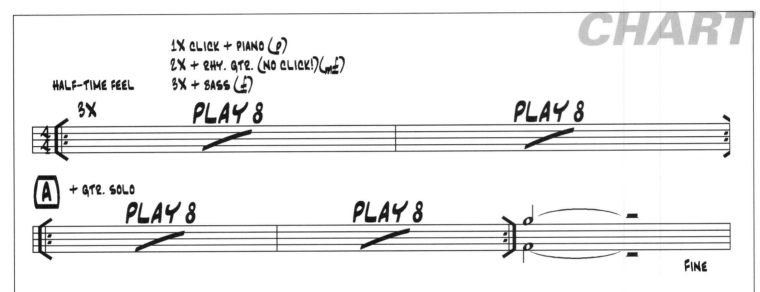

CHART

Groove 9 introduces a half-time feel. Half-time feels are important to get a handle on, both musically and visually. Visually speaking, I am referring to the chart. With the backbeats on beat 3, the music flows by faster than it would if they were written on beats 2 and 4. Hardly a big deal, but one of which you should be aware. Musically speaking, getting comfortable with and conceptualizing the backbeat on 3, is a crucial step in gaining control of the half-time groove, an infinitely useful tool. The DVD has a complete demonstration of half-time feels, so check it out if you are unsure of the concept.

This song reminds me of something Eric Clapton would write. I think he'd like these chords and the slowness of the groove. Our guitarist, Kevin Kuhn, indulges our Clapton-esque vibe by playing a beautifully lyrical solo starting at Letter A. You get a click the first time through to conceptualize where things lie within the confines of a metronomic pulse, but you get it only once, and then you're on your own. When that click drops out, you really appreciate the amount of space in this song that you are expected to bridge musically.

It's so nice to play this slow groove after the very athletic events of the sixteenth-note grooves at fast tempos. However, at slower tempos, you have to concentrate even harder on the time, and this song has so much space that if you zone out for even a microsecond, you're done. Variation A is, I think, an even better choice for this song than the main groove; it's simpler and fits just perfectly. Ah, but Variation B brings an intentional rub in the second bar against the bass line and that is great too . . . decisions, decisions.

ROCK

Groove 9 FAST Track 18

Variation A

Variation B

CHART

HALF-TIME FEEL   1X POWER TRIO!   3X - 4X + LEAD GTR.

2X + KEYS

4X   PLAY 16   FILL!

(BRIDGE)   PLAY 8   FILL!   PLAY 8

FINE

Crunchy! Crunchy guitars, crunchy bass; it sounds great, but it's a thick soup that will leave you grasping for the time if you aren't solid in the first place. Let's say you try this track and you get separated from the band. Don't despair! Listen to the track a few times *without* playing along. Then, try just tapping your hi-hat part softly with the music to understand how your part relates to the rest of the band. Then try adding the snare; then add the bass drum. This method of breaking the groove down to the hi-hat part and adding each limb separately is a great way to solve any problems.

The chart itself has no new elements and is straight-ahead; it's all about counting and knowing where you are. (Ding! Are you recording yourself?) Variation A has an active bass drum part, and I love how it feels with this song. I wouldn't use it for the entire song, but it's great to throw in at the end of the phrase just before a fill. Variation B has a half-time hi-hat part on top of the half-time snare and bass drum parts. For some reason, this simple-looking groove is a coordination killer. It's funny how you can't tell what will throw a student a curve-ball, but for some reason, this groove makes most drummers very uncomfortable with the coordination. If it stinks today, work it into submission tomorrow. It still stinks? There's always the day after that. Don't give up!

Groove 10 SLOW Track 19

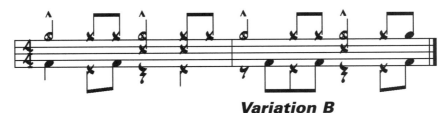

Variation A   **Variation B**

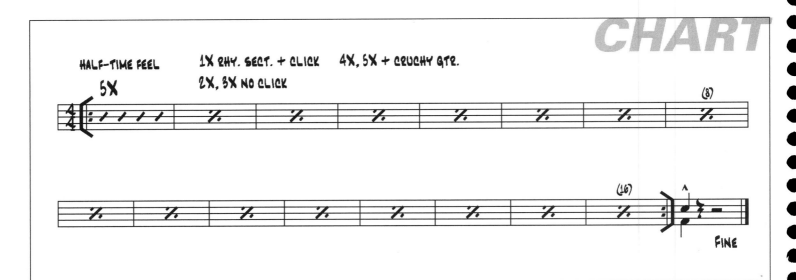

CHART

HALF-TIME FEEL   1X RHY. SECT. + CLICK   4X, 5X + CRUCHY GTR.

5X   2X, 3X NO CLICK

FINE

From a purely technical point of view, Groove 10 presents a more sophisticated approach to groove construction and is more spread out over the drumset. However, make no mistake; the ride pattern with its cutting bell on beats 1 and 3 are your focus and what binds the groove together. As with all these grooves, and everything else you do on the drums, *slow it down if you have problems!* Are you flamming? Are you rushing any of the internal parts? These are the important questions to ask now.

Half-time feels naturally gravitate toward a more open approach due to the fact that the grooves have more space and air in them. Leaving a little space in grooves is a fantastic thing, but you have to understand that, especially at slower tempos, the tendency is to cheat that space of its full value, creating an unsettled groove that rushes. How do you not rush? Simple—inside your head, you should be hearing *all* the subdivisions, *all* the time, even if you aren't playing them. So, even if you aren't playing all the eighth notes in a groove like this, you are *hearing* them and acknowledging their rightful value.

The first three times through the form illustrate just how much space all the musicians leave in half-time grooves. You are generously provided a click the first time through, but that's it, amigo. After that, you are on your own. The first few attempts may not go so well—don't panic! Stay rhythmically tight; don't hunt for the time, and don't go fishing for the groove. *Hear* the subdivisions in your head, the music in your ears, and lay it down.

If you are having problems with this groove, play Variation A. If you are ready for something different, try Variation B, which is an example of a groove/fill. I wouldn't play B through the entire song and neither should you; but when the guitar kicks in and things get hot, instead of playing the usual run around the toms (boring!), try throwing in Variation B which intentionally rubs against the groove and has a flurry of activity on the ride/hi-hat, not the drums. It works great until the tattooed shirtless singer shouts, "Dude, I like tom fills, dude! Play more toms, dude!" It's all part of the job.

ROCK
Groove 10 FAST Track 20

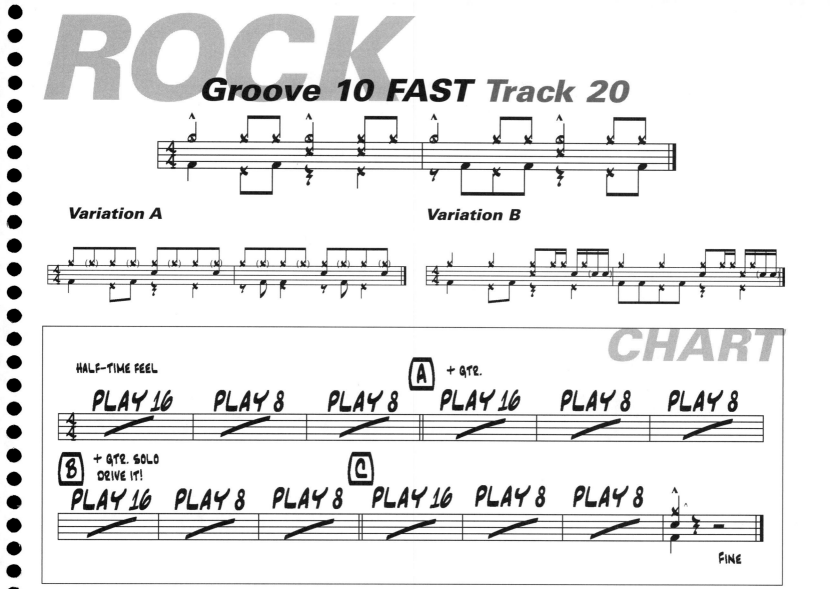

Variation A

Variation B

CHART

HALF-TIME FEEL

PLAY 16   PLAY 8   PLAY 8   [A] + GTR.   PLAY 16   PLAY 8   PLAY 8

[B] + GTR. SOLO
DRIVE IT!
PLAY 16   PLAY 8   PLAY 8   [C] PLAY 16   PLAY 8   PLAY 8

FINE

"Groove 10 Fast" is the same harmonic construction as "Groove 10 Slow," but played with a completely different intent. It also features the biting edge of an acoustic piano and a mean-sounding 5-string bass. You can hear the increased energy pouring out of the musicians at this tempo and how the time sits more forward than in the previous groove. That's the gloriously human thing about groove playing: Every tempo, every song, every instrument, and every musician brings their own interpretation of where their part sits inside the groove. When you listen to a track like this (which is just a power quartet of bass, piano, guitar, and *you*), it's easy to see how the parts interact; for instance, how quickly the piano speaks, and how the distorted guitar speaks slower but takes up so much more room on the track. You can imagine how you are going to line your bass drum up with the bass part and where the bass player is feeling the time. Then *you* come in, and everyone says you are doing it wrong! Part of the job . . .

The chart shows us that we're playing a 32-bar form four times through—no surprises. Variation A is fun to play, because we're ghosting all the upbeats on the ride. (For beginners, any notes in parentheses are *ghosts*, meaning that they're played very, very softly). Be careful here as in the main groove because of the coordination aspects required, which are a little tricky. Variation B works as a main groove or as a throw-it-in-once-in-awhile spice. The slick little paradiddle-based idea at the end of the groove creates some double-time motion, and if it is placed exactly in the pocket, sounds great. As always, feel no pressure to play it today if it doesn't yet feel right.

Chapter 2
FUNK Grooves

The term "funky" first appeared as a musical descriptive around the mid-1950s in connection with soul music and many people specifically credit the legendary session drummer, Earl Palmer, with its first use in this context. The roots of funk come directly from black soul music, gospel and rhythm andblues. These are big subjects, so please don't mistake this short synopsis for a complete tutorial.

In 1965, James Brown recorded the hit "Papa's Got a Brand New Bag," which established funk as a category in its own right. Though there were other significant funk artists, James Brown literally brought funk, funky beats, and the concept of funky R&B into the mainstream like no one before him. Funk has always fought an uphill battle for respect. The record companies didn't call Mr. Brown a funk artist; he was R&B, a category (like jazz) that still today adopts artists who aren't easily labeled. For most musicians, funk, even now, is more a concept than a distinct category. Funky rock, funky jazz, funky R&B—whatever—if you're funky, you're in the club.

In the 1970s, funk and rock started co-mingling (another constant in musical evolution is that no genre is above borrowing from its neighbors), and bands like Parliament (P-Funk), led by the inimitable George Clinton, were born. Jazz artists were not immune from funk, as made apparent by artists such as Herbie Hancock, beginning with his iconic *Head Hunters* recording. In the 1980s and beyond, Prince has shown his genius for rhythm. His knowledge of funk and his prolific production concepts are simply incredible. He is an example of a musician who understands past history and uses it to create the future. Currently, you find funk and funk-like influences everywhere. Hip-hop producers have made James Brown the most sampled musician in history, giving Mr. Brown's two main drummers, Clyde Stubblefield and John "Jabo" Starks, the wide recognition they so deserve.

We'll look at three different funk grooves that epitomize the syncopated (shifted accent) signature of funk in general. Just remember that Groove 1 in this book is a funk groove too! Sometimes, the drums groove simply while the other musicians "funk it up." Other times, the drums are active and the other musicians play simply. How do you know what to play? Simple—you listen.

Here's a list of funky people to get you going. First, see the movie *The Funk Brothers*, which provides an inside look at the groove makers from the Motown era.

A Few Funky Artists	Herbie Hancock (*especially Head Hunters and Thrust*)	Tower of Power	Dennis Chambers
James Brown		Soulive	Bernard "Pretty" Purdie
Maceo Parker	Prince	Galactic	Zigaboo Modeliste
Bootsy Collins	Ohio Players		Melvin Parker
Sly and the Family Stone	The Time	**A Few Funky Drummers**	Gregg Errico
The Meters	John Scofield (*Loud Jazz, Blue Matter, Electric Outlet*)	Clyde Stubblefield	Rick Marotta
Parliament		John "Jabo" Starks	Omar Hakim
Funkadelic	Cameo	David Garibaldi	
Bernie Worrell		Mike Clarke	

FUNK

Groove 11 SLOW Track 21

Variation A **Variation B**

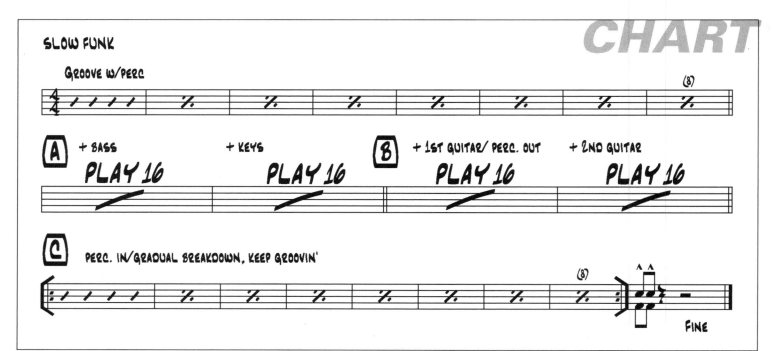

Okay, time to lay on the funk and make things greasy. You're going to have ample opportunity to get your funk on in this and all the funk songs, because every part is serving the groove in one form or another. "Groove 11 Slow" starts with just drums and congas, giving you the chance to focus on anything in your playing that isn't sitting in the pocket. As the rest of the band comes in layer by layer, listen closely to each instrument and how they react to the time. Do you hear how the bass is a little fatter than the guitar, which is more forward than the keyboards? Glorious! This is what makes music human. Your job is to find that perfect pocket (it's *so* there, trust me) and drive the band home. It'll be easy to do with the percussion player, but, once again, he takes a 32-bar break at Letter B, and you're on your own.

No surprises in the chart; just be aware that the groove breaks down around you over the last 16 bars while you keep grooving right through it. Variation A is a different take on syncopating (shifting the accent) the bass and snare parts, but the syncopation is a little simpler than in the main groove. Variation B is one of my favorites; it features the hi-hat playing the classic open-closed riff all by itself in the second bar. We talked about creating rhythmic tension previously and this is another instance where you can create some rhythmic mischief by leaving *space* instead of using notes.

42

FUNK

Variation A

Variation B

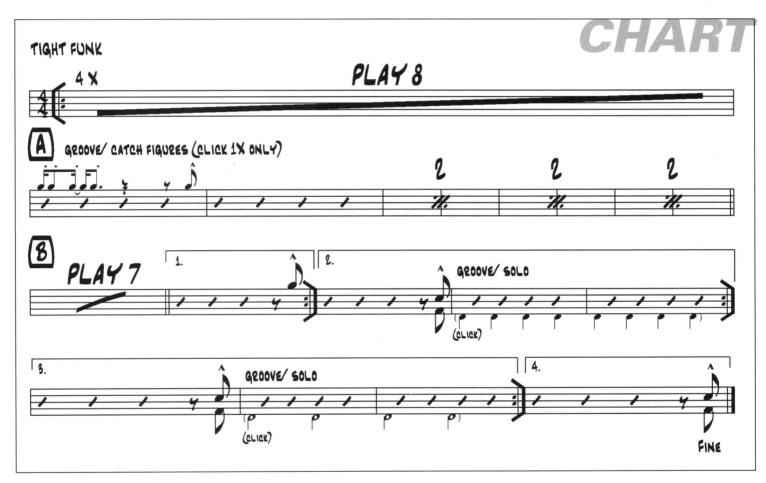

This track is musically busy from all the musicians. There is nothing wrong with busy grooves *if* the music calls for it. As with all matters of groove; it's in *how* you play busy. I constantly preach, "Simple, simple, simple!" That's truly good advice for many situations, but not all. Think of busy grooves like a sharp knife: Handle with care. Here's a short list to check if you want to play a busy groove with a live band:

- ■ **Internal dynamics (Is the volume balanced between all parts?)**
- ■ **Rhythmic clarity (Are all the beat subdivisions accurate inside the groove?)**
- ■ **Ensemble awareness (Do you know how each part reacts with the other band members' parts?)**

Honestly, this short basic checklist asks *all* the questions you need to know about all grooves. Of course the big question is always: "Is this groove serving the song?" but if I haven't made that clear by now, then I should write a book on baking. A new chart element appears at Letter A: the 2-bar repeat. The first two bars of Letter A are written out and then the following symbols tell you to *repeat the previous two bars*. Variation B is a very advanced groove that uses a linear concept and mixes open position (left hand on hi-hat) and closed (right hand on hi-hat).

43

FUNK
Groove 12 SLOW Track 23

Variation A   **Variation B**

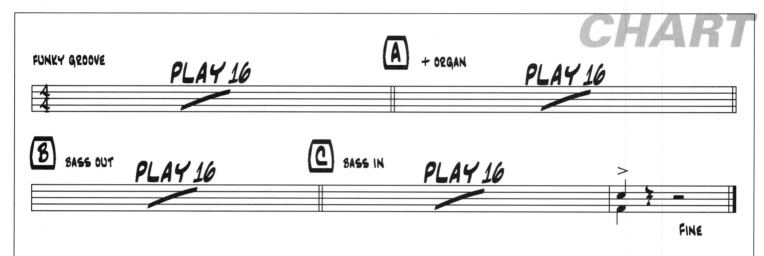

The New Orleans band called The Meters (currently called "The Funky Meters") is synonymous with no-frills gritty funk. Their classic lo-fi recordings capture a raw hardness that has earned them a place in the groove pantheon. "Groove 12 Slow" is our tribute to them. When you listen to the track with headphones, notice the two classic funky guitar parts: the left side has a "chicken pickin'" single note line, and the right side has a funky strum part. The bass and drums (even with their busy parts) wind their way through these lines tying them together.

The chart is straight-ahead: 16-bar phrases throughout. At Letter B you'll have a great opportunity to play around with the groove if you wish. The bass drops out leaving you alone to jam with the guitars and keys. By all means, if you wish to simply groove through, then go for it. But, if you are feeling adventurous, you can get into all sorts of mischief that will result in one of two things: a self-indulgent mess or a phenomenally slick groove section. Guess which one we want to aim for? Advanced players can switch from closed to open position and try some linear ideas, as well as adding grace notes, or conversely, leaving more space. The options are up to you; see what kind of trouble you can get yourself into. Don't worry, nobody's listening . . . for *now*! (cue: evil laughter . . .)

Because I'm such a nice guy, I gave you a click for the first 8 bars of the chart to get you settled in the groove. This will help those new to funk to understand what the heck is going on; it can be confusing at first. Variation A is a groove with the classic open hat sound on bar 2 and a sweet 7-stroke roll to get us back to the beginning. The main groove for both Groove 12 charts avoids the backbeat on beat 2; Variation B is another, yet completely different, way to get the same effect.

FUNK
Groove 12 FAST Track 24

Variation A   **Variation B**

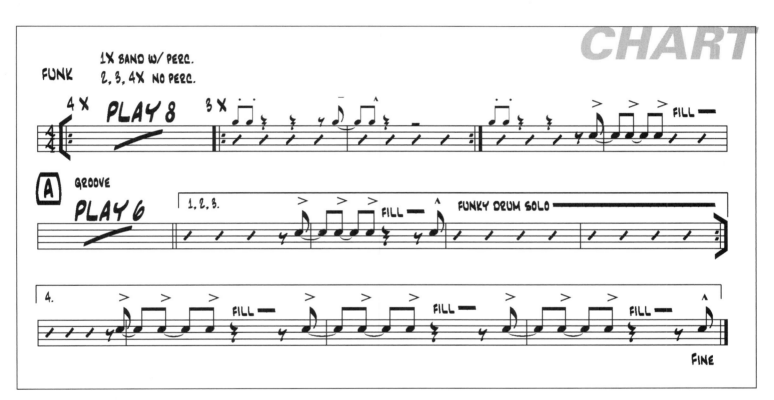

Let's start by talking about a feature common to the three fast funk songs in this book: a busy first 8 bars, with an ensemble figure for the next 8 bars. Look at the chart above to see what I mean. In "Groove 12 Fast," after the first 8 bars of groove, there is a 2-bar figure repeated three times (6 bars), followed by bars 7–8, which differ slightly from the 2-bar figure. As we learned before, we always observe the "repeats within repeats," so we play the figure three times when we come to it. Then, after we play our ensemble figures, we head right back into the groove.

Uh-oh, here's a "funky drum solo"—you know what that means, right? Go nuts! Just go nuts, hit everything you can and forget about the groove! *YES!!!* Is my sarcasm coming through? Good. In all seriousness, beginners should feel fulfilled by simply grooving through these 2 bars. For those up to the challenge, play a funky solo, but, remember that after your little solo, the band comes back in, so please, whatever you do, don't lose the groove. Your job is to connect the sections together and make it feel great. Don't drop the ball . . .

Variation A is close to the groove I play on the DVD for this tune, and it's a better choice than the main groove for this particular song. You see? You have to use your ears and do what's right for the piece, not get locked into what you *think* you have to play. Variation B is great for that ensemble figure we just talked about; it rubs against the figure, but also connects through the ensemble. Give it a try and see how it works for you.

FUNK

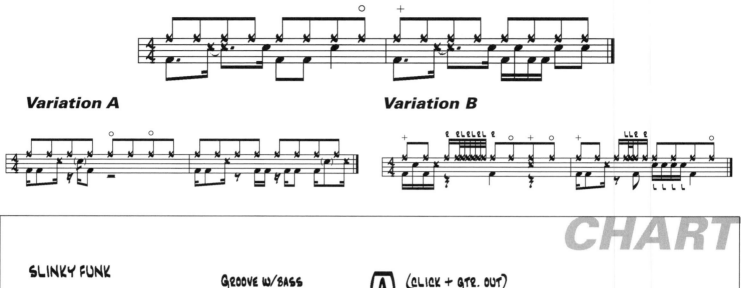

Variation A   **Variation B**

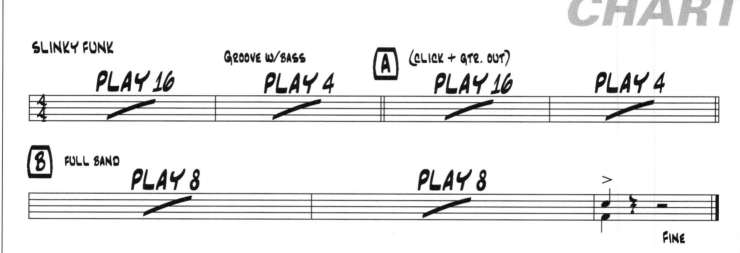

This groove has an intentionally displaced second beat. This is a very useful and common kind of funk groove that actually was used on the majority of songs in *The Lion King*. It's interesting how grooves that you might call "funk" can wind up in pop music if they happen to work with the songs. The moral of the story is: Don't get too into labels; if it works, it works.

You'll sometimes hear musicians refer to this groove as the "stutter," because of its lopsided feel. The song that we wrote for this groove illustrates how infectious this feel is; all the musicians were jumping on that displaced backbeat, except, of course, the guitarist, who was so far back in the pocket that we would have needed a crane to get him out. I love the part he plays (on beats 3 and 4 of every other bar); it's the perfect complement to the displaced beat in the front part of the bar. Tension and release . . . remember? Oh, and you only get a click up to Letter A. Hey, sorry, have you seen the price of clicks lately?

The variations are interesting alternatives to the main groove. Variation A mirrors the guitar on beats 3 and 4 with the open hi-hat sound. Variation B is a challenging groove that features some intricate hi-hat work and unexpected snare and bass drum interplay. I suggest slowing Variation B way down until it starts to sound like something resembling a groove, and then try throwing it into the tune as a spice at its original, faster tempo. This is another of those variations that makes a nice departure from the main groove once in awhile, but you wouldn't want to build a whole song on it.

FUNK

Groove 13 FAST Track 26

Variation A

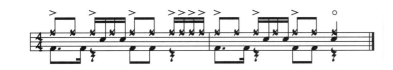

Variation B

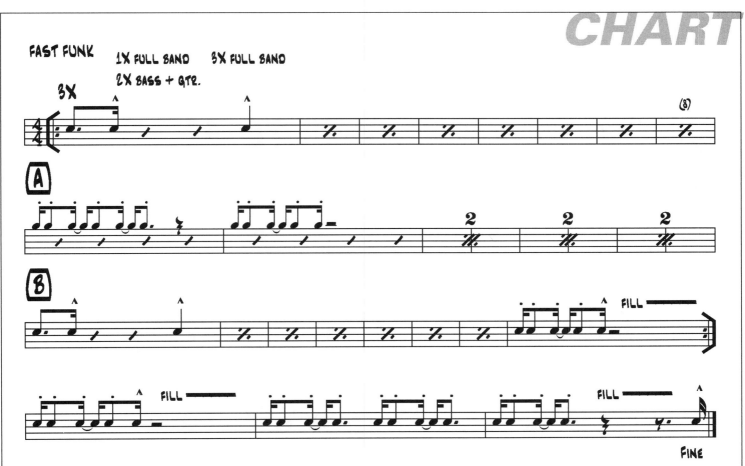

The sound of the guitar rhythmically strumming through the groove gives this track its signature sound. If you want to hear how drums and guitars work together, I have one name for you: James Brown. That pretty much says it all if you have any interest in funky grooves and dissecting funky groove construction.

Once again we have our buddy the 8-bar groove followed by the 8-bar ensemble figure: a classic sound in funk songs. This ensemble rhythm is by far the most syncopated and needs to be handled with care. Please don't beat the ensemble figure to death; rather, play through it, featuring the figure in your groove. Keep in mind that ensemble figures aren't drum solos (unless, of course, it says to solo over them), so commitment to the groove and time comes first.

Both variations presented are interesting alternatives to try. Variation A puts the displaced notes in the bass drum, and no backbeat is played until beat 4 of the second bar; that's a long time without a backbeat. Variation B opens with a ride cymbal and straight eighths chopping away with your foot on the hi-hat. Needless to say, coordination may be an issue here, so slow it way down if necessary.

DRUMSET KEY

CYMBALS ——— DRUMS ——— COWBELLS

RIDE CYMBAL · RIDE BELL · HI-HAT · HI-HAT OPEN · HI-HAT W/FOOT · BASS DRUM · BASS GHOST NOTE · SNARE · SNARE RIMSHOT · SNARE CROSS STICK · SNARE GHOST NOTE · TOM1 · TOM2 · FLOOR TOM · CHA-CHA COWBELL · COWBELL

Chapter 3
R&B and HIP-HOP Grooves

When discussing musical genres, R&B is probably only second to jazz in its diversity. There are so many styles referred to as R&B that to list even current artists would be a daunting task. So, rather than try to define the un-definable, let's talk about a little history and get our bearings.

The term "rhythm and blues" was coined in the late 1940s by record executives anxious to find another title for the increasingly popular "race music" being played by black Americans. During many musical evolutions, including R&B emergence, port cities were focal points for change with their influx of immigrants and the cultural influences brought with them. Particularly New Orleans, also a birthing place for jazz, had a huge impact on early R&B; this is one of the reasons that jazz and R&B are so tightly interwoven in both their history and commonality.

R&B was hardly confined to the United States. By the 1960s, the classic R&B sound had infected everyone including British rock artists such as the Rolling Stones, whose hits, particularly in the 1970s, were infused with an obvious love of R&B. Once again, we see the fusing of styles to create new and fresh music.

Today, the term "R&B" has taken on a very urban meaning. Radio stations and record companies use the terms "urban contemporary" and "urban pop" underneath the R&B umbrella to define many of today's popular R&B artists. In the 1990s in particular, R&B was hijacked by producers enamored with drum machines; thankfully, in the new millennia, that tide has started to swing back to using real musicians. In the list below, you'll see some artists who epitomize the R&B genre. Some are old, some are new, but all are the real deal. Obviously, this list is just to get you going. When you finish, go explore on your own . . . there's a lot of music to get turned on to.

Another trend lately amongst R&B artists is having killer bands with deadly drummers. John Blackwell, Aaron Spears, Eric Tribett, Nisan Stewart, ?uestlove, Gerald Heyward, and more are at the vanguard of a current crop of phenomenal young R&B drummers each with their own sound and pocket. The future looks good.

R&B ARTISTS

Babyface	Dr. John	Prince	Luther Vandross
Mary J. Blige	Alicia Keys	The Roots	Barry White
James Brown	Chaka Khan	Jill Scott	Bill Withers
Ray Charles	Gladys Knight	Take Six *(A capella with a great groove)*	Stevie Wonder
Earth Wind and Fire	John Legend		
Aretha Franklin	Brian McKnight	Tina Turner	
Marvin Gaye	The Neville Brothers	Usher	

Groove 14 SLOW Track 27

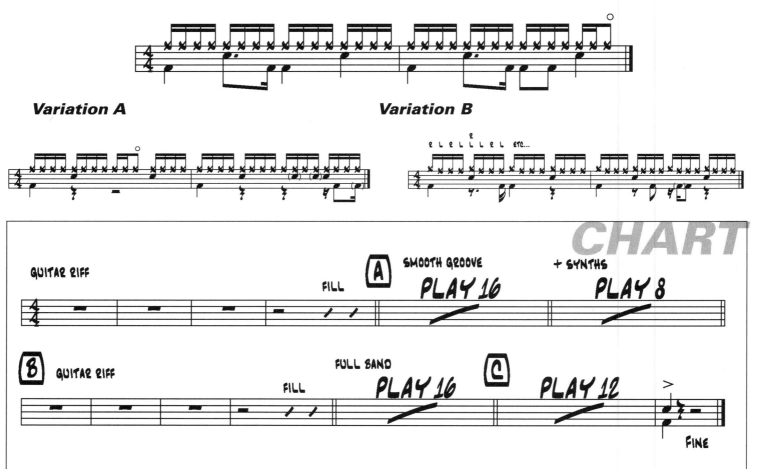

Variation A   **Variation B**

Starting with "Groove 14 Slow," we get to experience the different *feeling* I alluded to previously with the six-teenth-note rock grooves. Playing the hi-hat part with one hand, instead of two, gives the entire groove a different pocket. I find it fascinating that such a simple thing can change *everything* about a groove. The song itself is based on a catchy guitar *ostinato* (fancy Italian for a continuously repeating figure) and reminds me of an Earth, Wind and Fire track without the vocals. Together with the bass, you'll form a strong foundation for the guitarist to do his thing.

Variation A has the bass drum resting on beat 3, leaving a rather large gap with nothing going on but hi-hat. It can feel funny to go so long without playing your kick, but it's a great sound. Variation B is a classic groove inspired by the Steve Gadd vocabulary. Yes, if you want to get picky, it's played with two hands, but because of the constant motion from the hi-hat to the ride, it gives us a strong R&B feel that Steve used on so many great recordings in the early '80s. Check out Al Jarreau's classic album *Breakin' Away* to study the historic groove work of Mr. Gadd.

Groove 14 FAST Track 28

Variation A

Variation B

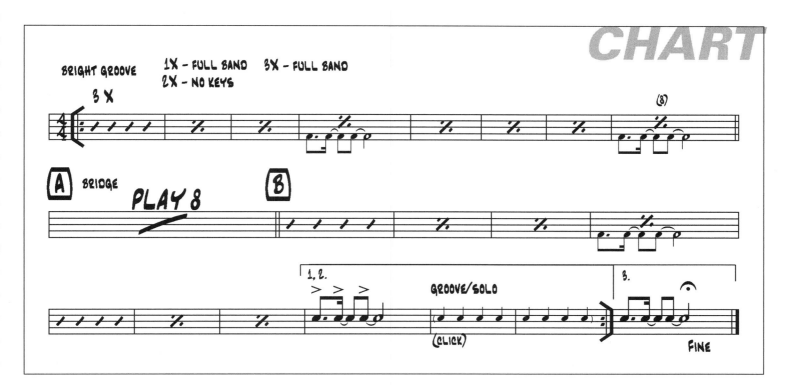

Man, it would be *so* easy to throw a ton of percussion on this track, with shakers playing every sixteenth and tambourines on the backbeats screaming "Here's the time! Here's the groove! Follow me!" Uh, no. We don't do that here because it defeats the purpose. The pocket is right there and you'll find it. And, even better, you'll find it all by yourself, leaving you with a feeling of pride and confidence. And, if you don't find it today, you will tomorrow. It'll come . . .

Ready for some alphabet soup? Stay with me now. This song is based on one of the most common song constructions in popular music: the AABA form. On your chart, the beginning eight bars is the A section, which repeats, so we have AA. The bridge, or the B section, comes next at Letter A on the chart; then at Letter B is the last A section, finishing out the AABA form. Rocket science, I tell you!

This chart contains no surprises; however, the writer was kind enough to provide a little bass figure in bars 4 and 8. When you see this, you'll know that you probably want to play that rhythm on your bass drum; and indeed, that would be a wise musical decision.

In terms of technique (you *are* practicing your rudiments, right?), the sixteenths may cause problems. Variation A offers a way to play this groove without playing every note on the hi-hat. Variation B is a little more adventurous with some roll work interspersed with more snare/bass interplay.

Groove 15 SLOW Track 29

Variation A   **Variation B**

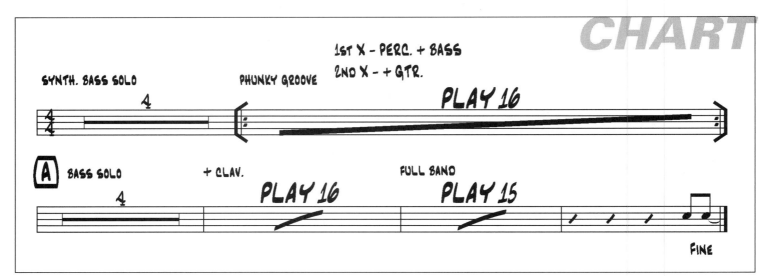

"Groove 15 Slow" is the one track in *Groove Essentials* that is built on loops and digitally manipulated audio. All parts were thrown up on a grid and moved around (quantized) to become "perfect." Some musicians lament technology and the use of loops and digital editing as do I when those tools are used to the detriment rather than the enhancement of the music. However, it's silly to debate the existence of technology; it's here to stay.

When playing with tracks that are quantized, you can do one of two things: Play perfectly yourself, or intentionally mess around with the pocket; play ahead of or behind the beat, or place the snare behind, or the kick drum in front, or the hi-hat behind . . . well, you get the idea. You can do as much experimenting with the pocket on this tune as you can with the other songs, but it's much easier since everything is so (new word invention, ready?) steriley.

This song is based on a common trademark of hip-hop music: a swing feel. The swing feel can be pronounced (tight) or subtle (loose). The DVD has a complete demo of this concept. Also, like many rap/hip-hop songs, there is no real form per se, but more of a jam concept. In a live R&B band, you'd probably rely on hand signals to stop, start, switch grooves, break it down, etc. The James Brown, Prince, and especially the late Frank Zappa bands are the masters at responding instantly to hand signals.

As explained in the DVD, the main groove uses all the elements of your kit to form the connective tissue of the groove. It's a tough one for coordination, so take your time. Modern R&B and hip-hop drummers love double-time fills and use them often. Variation A has a fast triplet figure in the bass drum, and Variation B is a *very* advanced example of a modern R&B quadruple-time fill. Don't hurt yourself.

Groove 15 FAST Track 30

Variation A **Variation B**

I love all the tunes in *Groove Essentials*, but if I were forced to choose the top five, "Groove 15 Fast" would make the list. It's a more improvisational approach to an R&B groove based on a song that just begs to be explored.

Let's talk about some new chart elements. This chart has many *cues* (small figures written above the staves that cue us into rhythms played by the band; we can play them or not—the composer lets us decide). The strange-looking second half of line 1 is a 4-bar repeat, telling us to repeat the previous 4 bars. Lastly, extra instruction is given at Letter A to repeat those 8 bars the last time.

Variation A is another approach to this feel, but played on the hi-hat with a stick, while Variation B is a more open example with an active hi-hat part played by the foot.

Groove 16 SLOW Track 31

Variation A   ### Variation B

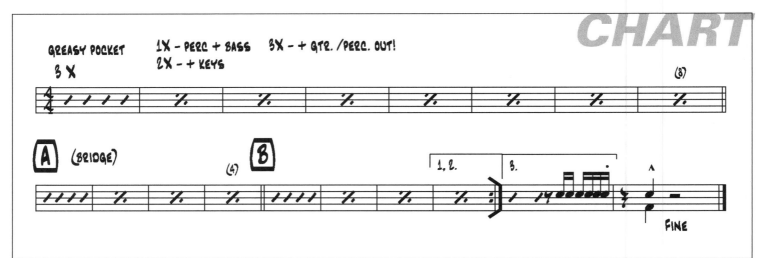

The hi-hat in Groove 16 has a much more pronounced effect on the overall pocket than it does in Groove 14. Whereas we want the hi-hat in 14 to be smooth, we want the hi-hat in 16, with its strong accents, to push the groove forward. This brings an eighth-note focus to the front although we're still playing all the sixteenths. This sound is a hallmark of great R&B drumming.

This hi-hat sound is very elusive for many drummers. Two common things may happen that you should avoid at all costs: losing rhythmic clarity and playing too loud. This is a good time to remind everyone that volume from the drums doesn't come from brute force; it comes from using smart technique. Playing too hard on this groove just kills it dead. The rhythmic clarity starts to suffer when the accents kidnap the internal taps (unaccented notes), forcing them out of place. If the sixteenths aren't perfect, regardless of accents, then stop, slow it down, figure it out, and only when it's fixed, try to play it at your tempo goal. No rush—enjoy the journey.

"Groove 16 Slow" gives you loads of space to find a place for your hi-hat. We'll play with some percussion in the beginning to help you find that sweet spot, but then you're on your own again. There are no surprises in the chart— you guys are old pros at multiple endings by now. Variation A features some different snare and bass drum phrasing, and Variation B offers a more rhythmically subtle construction with no backbeat on beat 2.

Groove 16 FAST Track 32

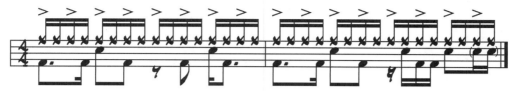

Variation A

Variation B

CHART

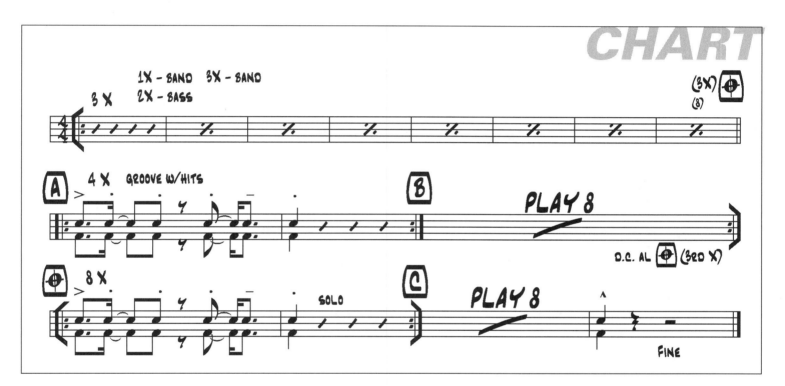

"Groove 16 Fast" is a super-tight track that has a few surprises. First, we see there is a new chart element called *D.C. al Coda* (⊕). First, two definitions:

- **■ *D.C.* (Da Capo): from the beginning, or literally, "from the head"**

- **■ *Coda* (⊕): the last section of music, or literally, the "tail"**

So when you get to the end of line 2 on the second repeat, go back to the beginning and play to the Coda sign (at the end of the line 1), then immediately jump (skipping over line 2 entirely) to the Coda sign on line 3 and play to the end—simple.

Musically, this song has a lot of space with no click, which is what *Groove Essentials* is all about. Listen, without a click, you are going to make many mistakes on this chart, but that is how you discover your time tendencies. Some of you will rush, some will drag, but the important thing is you'll discover what your natural weaknesses are and fix them. Hey, I've gone too long without asking an important question: Are you recording yourself?

Groove 17 SLOW Track 33

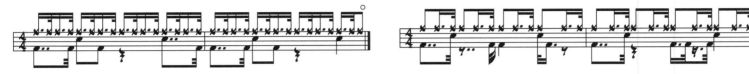

Variation A   **Variation B**

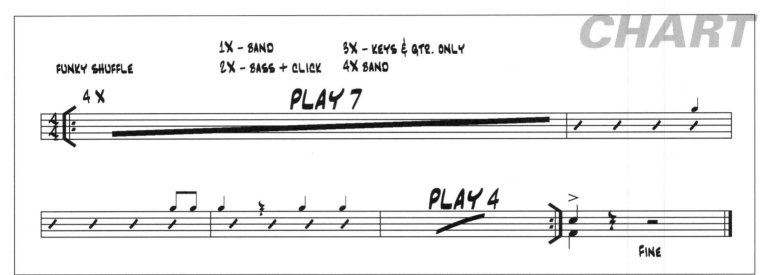

Ah, the classic half-time shuffle, a groove that every complete drummer should know. Two drummer icons have made this groove their signature: Bernard Purdie, from an R&B perspective; and the late Jeff Porcaro, from a more rock-oriented approach. In many circles, this groove is even called the "Purdie shuffle."

The main groove is simply one of hundreds of variations on a half-time shuffle. The common element for all the variations is the swing shuffle feel on the hi-hat. Again, with all things swing—jazz, blues, shuffles, hip-hop, etc.—your ride beat (in this case the hi-hat part) determines the swing factor for the entire band. I can't stress this enough: *Be consistent!* There is nothing more annoying to other musicians than a drummer who can't make up his/her mind on where the feel is (except, of course, a singer who insists on playing a shaker during ballads). Why, why, why do they do that?

Variation A is a great choice for this song since it has a little more space than the main groove. Variation B combines a slightly less busy hi-hat part with a displaced backbeat, borrowed from the syncopation ideas of the funk section. See? Mix and match, and come up with your own grooves, too.

Groove 17 FAST Track 34

Variation A

Variation B

The phenomenal pianist, Joe Sample, made landmark recordings under his own name, as well as with the Jazz Crusaders for over 20 years. Like other musicians in the late 1960s, he loved John Coltrane *and* Marvin Gaye. The music they made was a classic blending of both the R&B and jazz genres. "Groove 17 Fast" is our tribute to this classic sound.

Both variations presented are worth getting a handle on. Variation B is the classic ghosted snare part that all drummers love to play. Every internal beat of every triplet is covered, but the trick is dynamics; play the internal parts too loud and you have a silly-sounding mess on your hands. The forward propulsion of this groove is phenomenally powerful; learning to play it well is time well spent. Variation A assigns straight eighths on the hi-hat, while all the other internal parts are still swinging. This is a great option when things feel too thick and busy. Subtraction in groove construction is as powerful a tool as addition.

Once again, we have a riff that has no click to help you at Letter A. Sorry. I do this because I care. Oh, all right, you get a click the first time through, okay? Man, I'm such a softy.

DRUMSET KEY

CYMBALS — DRUMS — COWBELLS

RIDE CYMBAL | RIDE BELL | HI-HAT | HI-HAT OPEN | HI-HAT W/FOOT | BASS DRUM | BASS GHOST NOTE | SNARE | SNARE RIMSHOT | SNARE CROSS STICK | SNARE GHOST NOTE | TOM1 | TOM2 | FLOOR TOM | CHA-CHA COWBELL | COWBELL

Chapter 4
JAZZ Grooves

As the *New* World, America got a bit of a late start; therefore there aren't many artistic inventions that can be called truly American. Jazz, however, is unquestionably America's indigenous art-form that, like all popular musical styles, has become part of the global fabric of the musical world. A study of jazz is also a study of American history: a story of people, passion, and life. Though it does little to explain the vibrant *present* of jazz, the Ken Burns' documentary *Jazz* is a great history lesson for understanding the evolution of jazz. I am not one for over-studying music history down to its minutiae, but a broad overview of how any music evolved, especially jazz, can help contemporary musicians to play with a broader scope of musicality.

I'm sure there are many drummers who arrive at the jazz section of any book, including *Groove Essentials*, with a sense of insecurity and dread. It isn't that you don't want to learn how to swing and play jazz—you do, that's why you're here. But, if you were born after 1965, you have a big obstacle to overcome that is easier to understand after you conceptualize it. Ready? Here we go . . .

Really, regardless of your cultural background (except for a few African, Middle-Eastern and Asian cultures), you've had straight eighth-note music banged into your head from the time you were born. There is no escaping it. It is literally all around you, because straight-eighth backbeat music is globally pervasive; you couldn't avoid it even if you tried . . . and more than a few have. Now, here comes jazz/swing—a music based on a much rounder feeling of triplets. It's foreign! I've seen this phenomenon for years: students struggling, through no fault of their own, to get a handle on swing. It's simply not, as my dad would say, "in their ears." So, how do you get it in your ears? How do you get *any* music in your ears? *Listen*, of course. Ah, but to what? Well, I've seen lists of recordings in books, but I know if *I* listened to them straight away with no jazz experience, I'd be more than a little confused. Jazz has a vocabulary that can be very advanced and implied, unlike most rock music that is more obvious and clear. For a first-timer, listening to Elvin with Coltrane is like teaching calculus to a fourth-grader.

Let it be known that the umbrella of jazz is huge! Jazz/rock, jazz/Latin, jazz/Brazilian, classic fusion, light jazz, acid jazz, be-bop, hard-bop, electric jazz, jazz/funk, swing, Dixieland, ragtime—the list is literally endless, because there is no music that hasn't been fused with jazz, and the reverse is also true. Now there are "jazz" bands with DJs, so the trend continues. But the root of jazz—the actual basis of what jazz is at its core—is swing. Mastery of the swing feel, combined with grooves from all the other chapters in this book, gives you the skills to explore all the various fusions that exist.

Many younger drummers don't even know if they *like* jazz, because they've rarely heard it. I've always considered it my job to get these students *excited* about jazz first; then we can talk about swinging.

So, what do you do? Where do you start? Two words: big band. Music for big bands (ensembles of about 12–18 musicians playing jazz) and swing music were at one time the popular styles of music in America and much of the world, making triplet-based music more common than straight-eighth style. Interestingly, the condition flows both ways; many jazzers had, and still have, a hard time playing straight rhythms without swinging them. To live in both camps with authority and comfort takes practice and an understanding of both the swing world and the straight-eighth world.

Big band, because of its ensemble approach and more structured musical parameters, appeals to many drummers coming from the straight-eighth world, where songs are sectionalized into easy-to-digest parts. They love the sheer power of the big band and the active, yet easy to understand, role the drummer plays in them. The alternative to big bands, speaking in terms of swing, is known as the small group; typically a trio to a sextet. As with big bands, these small groups can be musically structured, but the sheer size of big bands and the fact that the players are all reading from charts, makes big band music easier for beginners to digest than music for small groups. Also, it's just plain exciting to hear that many musicians playing together!

However, the best thing about big bands is how they incorporate the best of the small group; virtually every big band chart features a solo or "blowing" section where just the soloist and the trio (piano, bass, and drums) get to play like a small group. Right away, a beginner playing big band music will experience:

■ **Tightly-arranged music that is easy to hear, discuss, and practice**

■ **Small-group playing in virtually every chart, usually with more than one soloist**

■ **Easily hear how different instruments, and groupings of instruments, play and feel swing**

Once students get a handle on some great big band music, they become excited about swing. From this point, it becomes infinitely easier to introduce them to small-group swing, and from there, of course, Elvin with Coltrane. So, if you are looking for someone to tell you music to buy, I will. These three CDs will get any drummer with a pulse excited about playing this incredible music. I practiced everyday after school with each of these recordings.

■ *Buddy Rich Big Band/Big Swing Face:* **Buddy at his glorious best in the 1960s, fearlessly recorded live. Forget about the incomparable facility for a minute; listen to the music—the driving swing and total command of the instrument.**

■ *Count Basie/Basie Big Band:* **Butch Miles plays great on this one, but I'm recommending it for its tight Sammy Nestico charts and the famous Basie swing. There's nothing like it.**

■ *Terry Gibbs Dream Band Vol. 5/"The Big Cat":* **Mel Lewis at his finest. Recorded live with an amazing band, amazing charts, and some of the most tasteful big band drumming you'll ever hear. Any of the Dream Band CDs are great, but Vol. 5 is my favorite.**

Now that you are sufficiently pumped-up about swing, let's get back to *Groove Essentials*. For the next 18 charts, you are going to be playing in a trio (piano, bass, and drums). The classic trio rhythm section is at the heart of most swing bands, large or small. So, to help you get ready to play along with your new big band CDs, we're going to get used to playing some solid, swinging time in a trio. If you are not sure how to begin, the DVD will help; I give in-depth explanations and demonstrations on how to play the classic swing beat. It's a lot easier to explain on the DVD than to write about it here.

Let's be clear about what jazz is and why it's unique. Jazz is an *improvisational* art, meaning that you make it up as you go along, responding to the music and the other musicians. So honestly, these aren't grooves in the same sense that a funk beat is a groove. Rather, the songs and motifs used with the following groove pages are concepts that will hopefully inspire you to reach out to this vast world we call jazz.

The term "comping" is used constantly in jazz, and it confuses many people, so we'll clear it up right now. As we swing in a rhythm section, we constantly play complementary rhythms with various limbs with the goal of propelling the swing forward. Playing these "comp"-limentary rhythms is called "comping." For example, we might play them with our left hand on the snare drum underneath the ride cymbal beat. We can also play them with our foot on the bass drum. We can even comp on the hi-hat by changing its rhythm around; however, you'll hear most comping coming from the bass drum and snare. The drummer isn't the only one comping; the piano player comps too while playing the chordal structure of the tune. Have a nice musical conversation with him/her.

On each page for every song for Grooves 18–22, you'll encounter five different comping ideas. The first two will be on the snare line while the next three ideas will feature some snare and bass interplay which could be a coordination red flag for some drummers; if so, slow it down. Remember, the idea is to *improvise off* the top of your head—no reading, no thinking—just use your ears and play music. This does not happen overnight and you must listen to great jazz drummers and analyze their comping to really have an idea of how to comp and improvise.

Below, I list some jazz drummer icons, young and old, who are worth listening to over and over again. Some are exclusively small-group musicians; some are big band, and some are both. All are masters of swing.

Jeff Ballard	Jack DeJohnette	Philly Joe Jones	Buddy Rich
Louis Bellson	Peter Erskine	Gene Krupa	Max Roach
Brian Blade	Billy Hart	Mel Lewis	Bill Stewart
Art Blakey	Roy Haynes	Lewis Nash	Ed Thigpen
Teri Lynn Carrington	Billy Higgins	Clarence Penn	Jeff "Tain" Watts
Jimmy Cobb	Elvin Jones	John Riley	Chick Webb

"The greatest contribution jazz has made in music has been to replace the role of the conductor with a member of the ensemble who, instead of waving his arms to keep time and convey mood, is an active member of the musical statement. That person is the drummer."

—Elvin Jones

JAZZ
Groove 18 SLOW Track 35

Comping Motifs

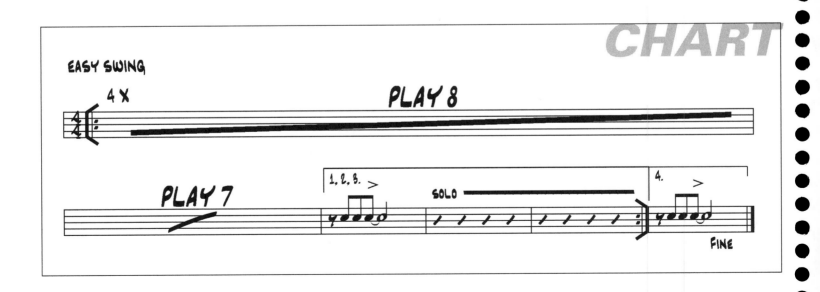

Groove 18 FAST Track 36

Comping Motifs

CHART

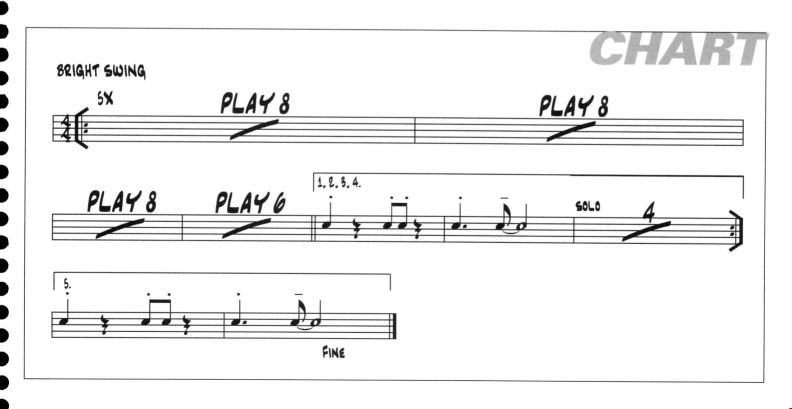

JAZZ
Groove 19 SLOW Track 37

Comping Motifs

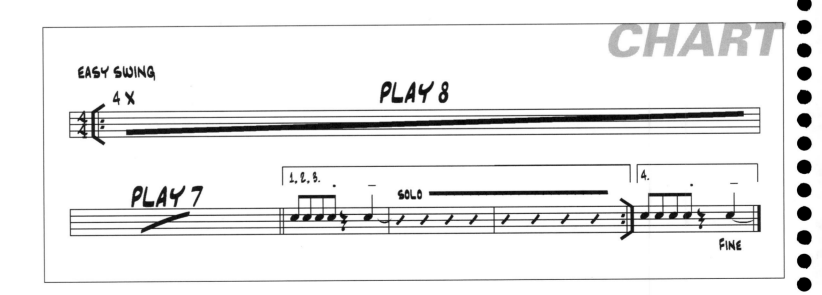

Groove 19 FAST Track 38

Comping Motifs

CHART

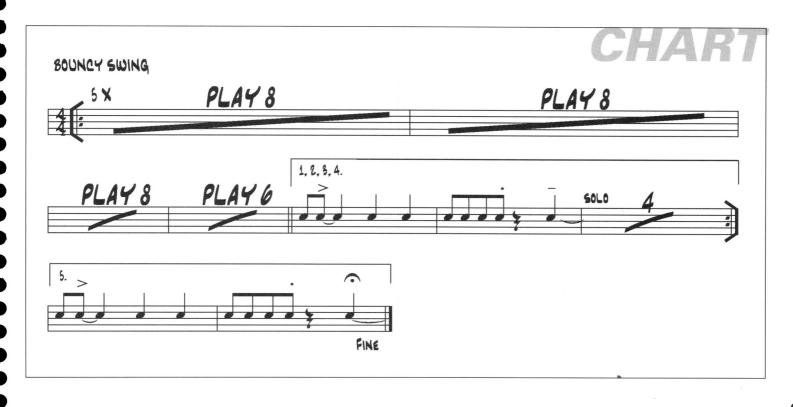

JAZZ
Groove 20 SLOW Track 39

Comping Motifs

LAZY SWING

FINE

JAZZ
Groove 20 FAST Track 40

Comping Motifs

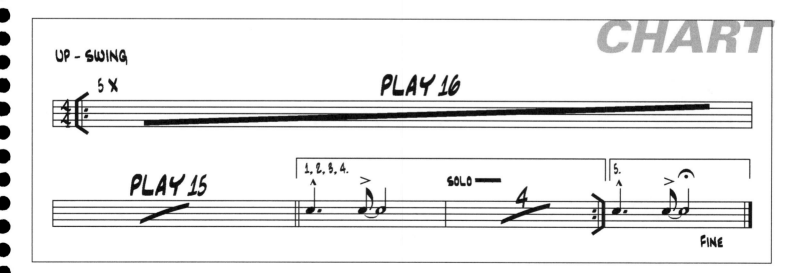

CHART

UP - SWING

5 X   PLAY 16

PLAY 15   1, 2, 3, 4.   SOLO ——   5.   FINE

JAZZ
Groove 21 SLOW Track 41

Comping Motifs

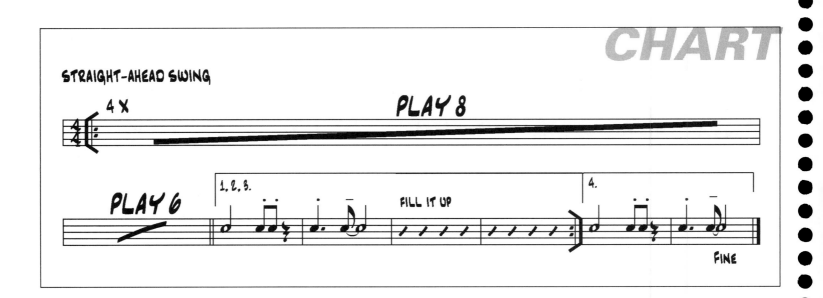

JAZZ

Groove 21 FAST Track 42

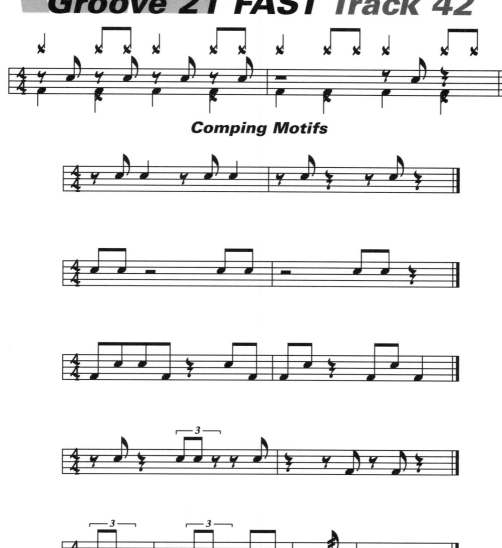

Comping Motifs

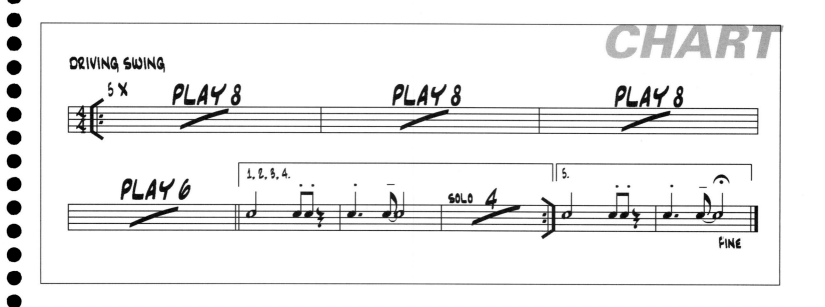

JAZZ
Groove 22 SLOW Track 43

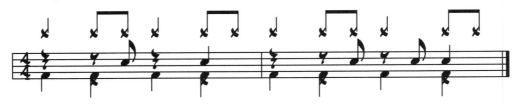

Comping Motifs

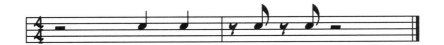

CHART

RELAXED SWING

Groove 22 FAST Track 44

Comping Motifs

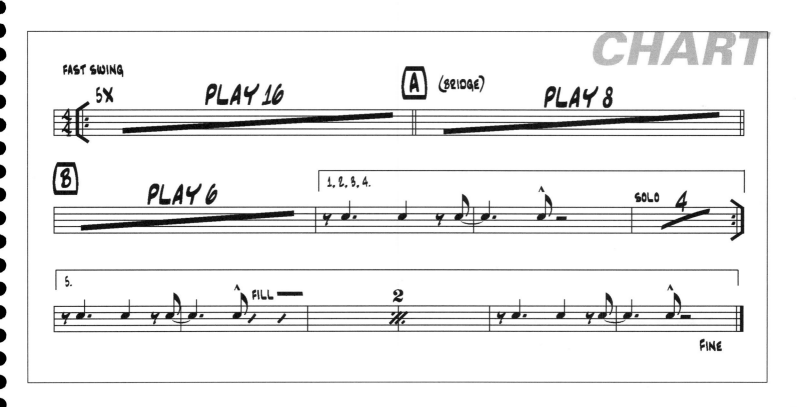

JAZZ
Groove 23 (Shuffle) SLOW Track 45

Variation A

Variation B

I can't think of a groove that I love to play more than a shuffle. I also can't think of a groove that has spawned more sub-grooves than the shuffle. And, of course, I can't think of a more important groove to know than a shuffle. Wow, that's some intro.; this better be good.

The classic shuffle has been around for a very, very long time. All sorts of camps take credit for *inventing* the shuffle, but it's pretty standard thinking to associate the earliest shuffles with blues artists from Chicago. In fact, the classic "chuh . . . guh, chuh . . . guh, chuh . . . guh, chuh . . . guh" rhythm was called the "Chicago shuffle." All the terminology for shuffles can get confusing, so in keeping with my keep-it-simple approach, when you hear the term "shuffle," simply think: Swing with some sort of backbeat. That, to be sure, is an oversimplification of what can be a diverse groove subset, but believe me; it all boils down to some sort of swing with a backbeat. Chicago plays it tight, the Cajuns play it loose (almost straight!), Memphis has a rolling lilt that is in the middle, Texas removes the ride cymbal playing it all on the snare, and, of course, New York knocks you to the ground, steals your wallet while snarling about how there is no such thing as a regional shuffle so stop talking so much and play some music, will ya? (So crabby, those New Yorkers.)

The chart is straight-ahead, no surprises. Variation A is a an old school shuffle with both hands playing *exactly* the same thing (a great sound!), and Variation B has a little syncopation in the bass drum. As always, if any of this leaves you confused, you know where to find the answers: the DVD.

JAZZ

Groove 23 (Shuffle) FAST Track 46

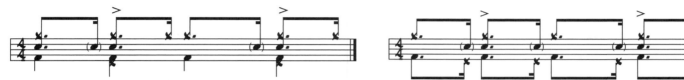

Variation A

Variation B

Here's a romping shuffle based on the classic 12-bar blues. So much music, jazz in particular, is built on this 12-bar progression, so pay attention to how it sounds and feels when you play this classic form. This will be a good time to remind everyone that all the rhythms of the entire jazz section are based on triplets no matter how they are written. Straight-eighths and dotted eighth-sixteenths are used in the variations, but everything should always swing like triplets. Why don't they just write triplets? Good question. Two reasons: First, jazz is interpretive, so even though triplets are a great place to start with your swing feel, they can be played looser or tighter depending on the tempo, so they aren't any more correct than eighths; second, eighths are a more professional approach to writing *interpretive* music like swing, since triplets written all over the page would be a cluttered mess.

Variation A *subtracts* some notes from the snare drum which is a very effective option when things feel too thick. Variation B has the hi-hat playing on the upbeats, a very slick sound. Needless to say, but I'll say it anyway: This variation has to be played perfectly or it'll sound like you're stomping grapes. You *are* recording yourself, right?

JAZZ
Groove 24 (2-Feel) SLOW Track 47

Variation A   **Variation B**

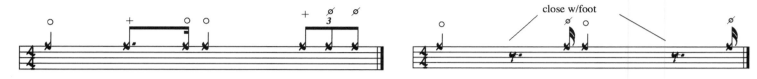

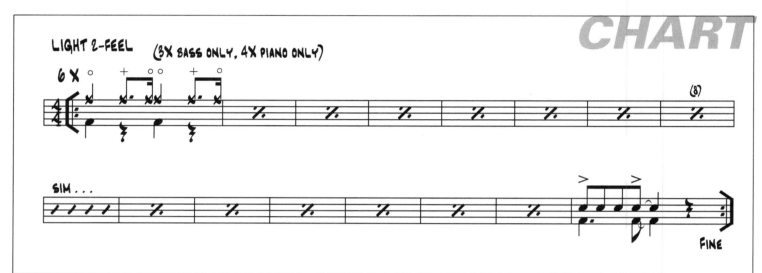

It's funny how a simple thing such as playing in "2" can cause such a fuss. Students practically *stop* playing when a chart says "2-feel," and I've figured out over the years why this happens. Playing "2-feels," as opposed to "walking 4-feels," almost always does three things: 1) Drops the intensity of the rhythm section down a few notches; 2) drops the volume down a bit, and; 3) adds much more space to the music and openness to the beat. That's a heck of big change, especially if it happens in the middle of a tune you've been playing in "4." It can feel like the bottom just dropped out from under you, so you must get even *more* intimate with the time, concentrating on keeping the rhythm section focused and together while you add more space to your playing! Seems like a contradiction, but it's not.

When you listen to great jazz drummers play in "2," notice that their commitment to the time is just as strong as when they play in "4." I want you to discover how to play in "2" on the hi-hat, something that Mel Lewis called "a lost art," so on these tunes, use that versatile sizzle hi-hat sound that I demo for you on the DVD. You can also play in "2" on the ride, which is a great choice at times. Additionally, when playing in "2," you can also lightly comp with your left hand. However, I recommend in the beginning, that you just enjoy playing your hi-hat and manipulating it with your hand, stick, and foot. Those three things can create a torrent of rhythm and color that is wondrous and impossibly slick. Variations A and B are examples of skewing the hi-hat rhythm ever so slightly. Remember, the hi-hat can either be a brush in the hand of an artist or two sheets of metal that clunk together. Decide now which hi-hat sound you want to create.

JAZZ

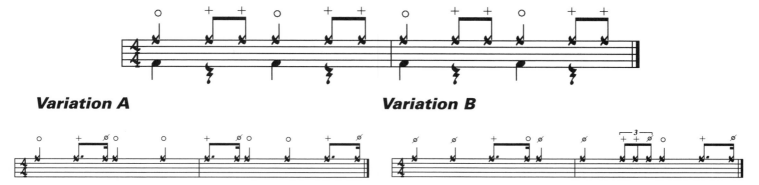

Variation A   **Variation B**

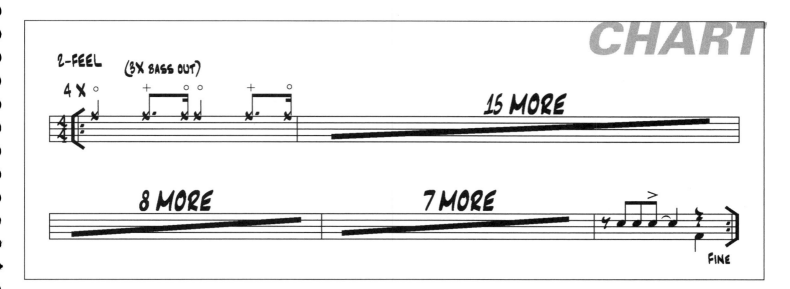

Here is a brighter version of playing in "2." Listen to the bass laying down those half notes so clearly and how the piano plays with a light touch as his rhythmic comping helps propel the swing forward. Our hi-hat joins the party with a light forward feeling as well.

Once again, playing the hi-hat like we do in this groove is mysterious for many drummers, particularly those of you coming from rock backgrounds. It's so different from everything else you've done before, and it's going to feel bizarre in the beginning. Remember the key word for success in learning new musical stuff: *Copy!* Sit down and play something you enjoy *exactly* like whomever you are trying to copy. I don't know why this isn't common sense, but to learn new things on an instrument, you have to try to exactly emulate what you are trying to learn. Then, and only then, can you make up your own stuff. And if you can't do this now, that's okay; do it tomorrow or the day after that.

So, remember those big band CDs I recommended? There is a lot of fine "2-feel" playing on these, so pick out some sections you like, and try to sound like one of those fine drummers. Variation A dances with the hi-hat rhythm, making it a little bit syncopated, while Variation B is a little more adventurous with a triplet that should be light and flow forward.

JAZZ

Groove 25 (Jazz Waltz in 3) SLOW Track 49

Variation A   **Variation B**

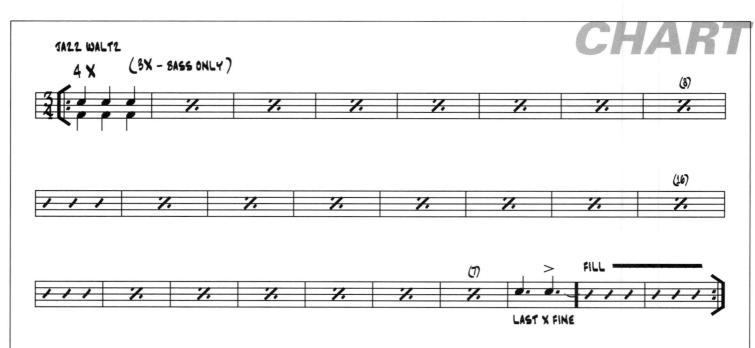

Our first jazz waltz is in "3," conveying the feeling of 3 beats per bar. Listen to the bass taking care of each beat, walking through the bars just as he does when playing the regular 4/4 swing. Our patterns and forward motion will bring that feeling of "3" to the forefront.

Variations A and B both represent different interpretations of playing in "3." You'll see eighths, dotted eighths, sixteenths, and triplets all mixed together on these variations, but they are all just "swing" notes, regardless of how they are written.

JAZZ

Groove 25 (Jazz Waltz in 3) FAST Track 50

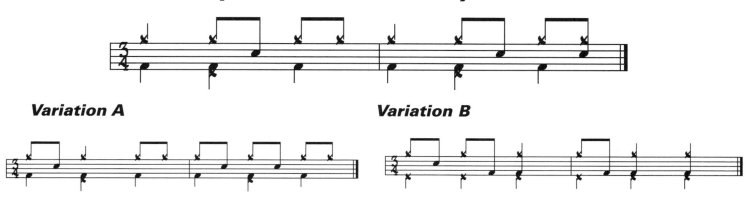

Variation A   **Variation B**

Explore this great jazz waltz in "3" and at a brighter tempo. Remember that the term "fast" is intentionally ambiguous. Fast here may be considered barely medium in some circles, or impossibly fast in others. Tempos, as with all things musical, are subject to interpretation. Variation A is a nice pattern that flows easily; Variation B has a little more interplay in the bass drum. Keep it smooth and flowing forward. Comping rhythms should always enhance, never hinder, the groove.

JAZZ
Groove 26 (Jazz Waltz in 1) SLOW Track 51

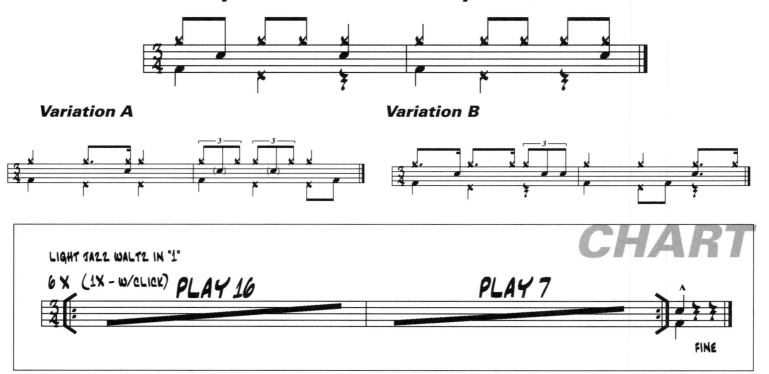

Variation A

Variation B

CHART

LIGHT JAZZ WALTZ IN "1"

6 X (1X - W/CLICK) PLAY 16   PLAY 7

FINE

Now let's explore Groove 25's close cousin, the jazz waltz in "1." In Groove 25, the bass walks on all the beats, but in this groove, only plays 1 downbeat per bar. Therefore, we must adjust our pattern accordingly to help convey the feeling of "1-ness."

I've put a click in for you the first time through the form because of the incredible amount of space that is now present. After that, you will be expected to keep the time by yourself. Isn't it amazing, when you listen to the track, how different this jazz waltz feels from the previous jazz waltz in "3"? Such small changes make a huge difference!

The chart is another one of those "um, don't knock yourself out or anything" charts. But, it has everything you need, and it gives you a very important piece of information. The last phrase is clipped by 1 bar, so it is only a 7-bar phrase instead of the usual eight. It feels funny to play that 7-bar phrase after playing in such symmetrically perfect phrase lengths for so long; but it's something to be aware of and able to navigate. It's not a big deal; just count to seven. See? Problem solved.

Both variations work beautifully with this chart as well as the main groove. Again, we see different notation with eighths and dotted figures mixed with triplets, but you know to just swing it all, no matter what it looks like on the page.

JAZZ

Groove 26 (Jazz Waltz in 1) FAST Track 52

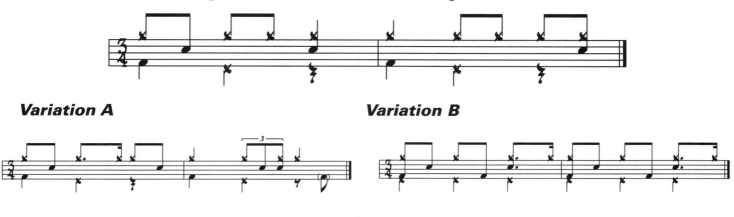

Variation A

Variation B

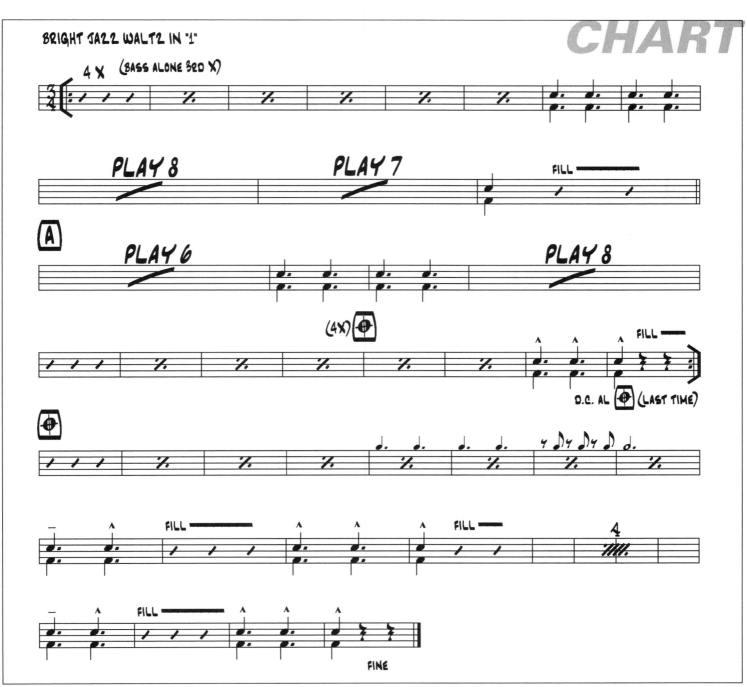

Here's our tribute to the classic playing of the great pianist McCoy Tyner. Mr. Tyner played with Coltrane and Elvin Jones on legendary recordings, and we would be remiss if we passed on the opportunity to give you a track that represents this classic sound.

Chapter 5
WORLD/Specialty Grooves

The world sections of the *Groove Essentials* poster, DVD, and play-along CD are rightfully the most populated. We're going to visit many countries and cultures in our exploration of global rhythms.

Here's a list of the places we'll be visiting in the world section:

- **Africa**
- **America**
- **Argentina**
- **Brazil**

- **The Caribbean**
- **Cuba**
- **Dominican Republic**
- **Jamaica**

- **Martinique**
- **Trinidad**

To discuss even one of these countries completely and explain the relationship between the culture and the music, not to mention the dense history of each place, would take more pages than this entire book. Therefore, it would be silly to suggest that *Groove Essentials* will be the final stop on your journey through these and other grooves. On the contrary, this is your launching pad, the place to get exposed to authentic music and drumming in a way that, hopefully, inspires the desire to know even more of the culture.

Again, the importance of culture cannot be overstated. The interweaving of the music with the food, drink, religion, and politics of each culture is as much a part of the music as, for example, understanding the clave in Afro-Cuban music. And now, with the information-packed Internet at your whim, all you have to do is type in a few words, and you're on your way to satisfying your curiosity about cultures new to you.

The world section was carefully constructed to ride the line between grooves that exist and grooves you'll actually need to play with bands. In many of the world grooves we'll be trying to emulate various world percussion instruments, but keep in mind that *Groove Essentials* is a drumset book written from a drumset perspective. Music that has no drumset, like flamenco, for example, is not discussed; but flamenco music is a complex rhythmic feast, and it can be very therapeutic to listen to music without drumset. Hindustani music from North India is another example of mind-bending rhythms that we, as drummers, may not get a chance to actually play often; but it's great to listen to, appreciate and, if possible, study.

Of course, nothing actually beats going to these places if that option is open to you. Traveling to experience the real culture and the music played by the real musicians who live the life every day, is a thrill. I've been lucky to travel almost every part of the globe, and, almost without exception, I've found local musicians and cultures very open and warm to students curious about their music. Learning world rhythms makes everything you do behind the drumset, regardless of what style you call "home," better.

WORLD

Groove 27 DISCO Track 53

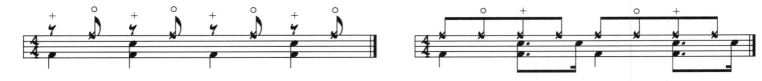

Variation A

Variation B

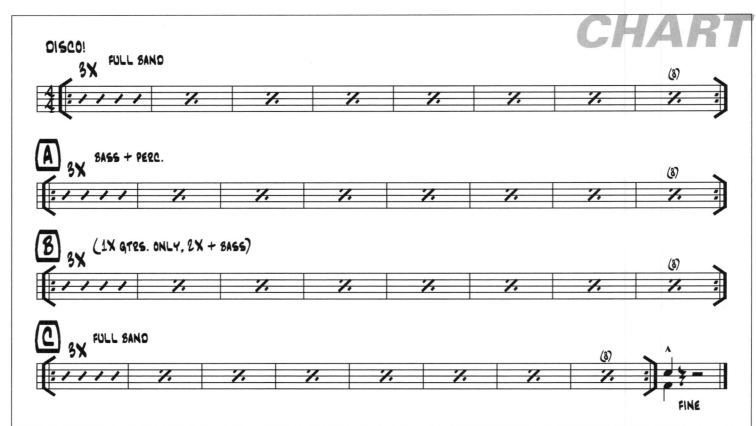

Finished laughing yet? Yeah, I know . . . when I first constructed the groove poster, more than a few eyebrows were raised, including mine, to see this groove in the world section. But there is a reasonable explanation: There ain't no place else to put it! I could have put it in the R&B section (which, by the way, disco is an official member of), or I could have even put it in the rock section, but I was afraid of death threats from the rock elitists out there—you know who you are. And then . . . it came to me. It's, it's, it's . . . a *specialty* groove! Yeah, that's it, it's a specialty groove. It has a nice ring to it.

Honestly, the groove is called "disco," but that doesn't really speak to its versatility. This classic groove is now used in so many different musical sub-genres that you hear it literally everywhere. Regardless of what you want to call it, it's a great groove—you don't even have to tell people it's a disco beat if you don't want to. It'll be our little secret.

WORLD

Groove 28 (Classic 2-beat) SLOW Track 54

Variation A　　　　　　　　　　**Variation B**

CHART

I can't overstate the importance of the classic 2-beat. This groove is literally anything you want it to be, hard rock all the way to, as with this song, a light Broadway-esque example.

WORLD

Groove 28 (Classic 2-beat) FAST Track 55

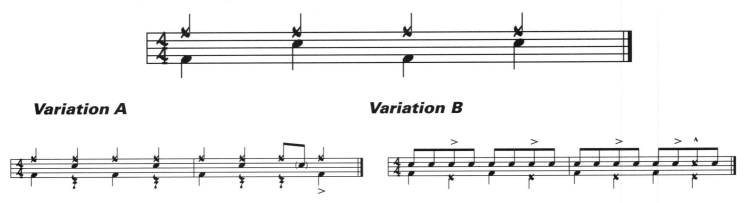

Variation A

Variation B

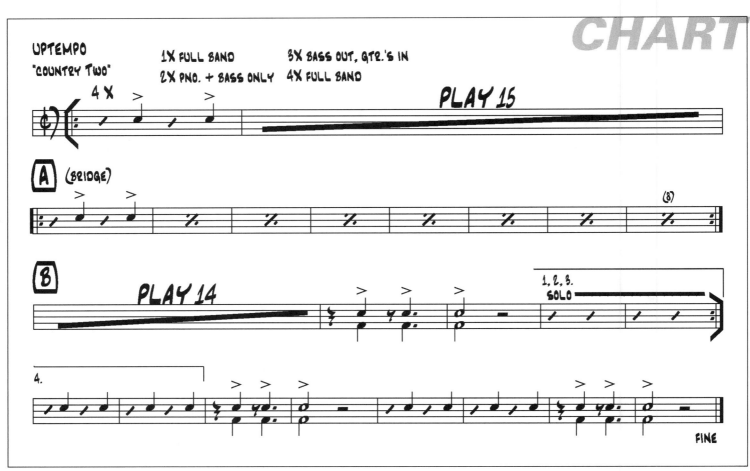

To illustrate the versatility of the classic 2-beat, here is an up-tempo song with a country flavor featuring two guitars and a banjo. Let them do all the fancy stuff, and we'll just keep the time. Somebody has to mind the store . . .

Variation A has a little skip at the end, which I've found to be a great technique to get the groove to "jump" a little bit higher when needed. Variation B is a little "chicken pickin'" pattern on the snare drum that provides a nice alternative to the traditional 2-beat sound.

Groove 29 (New Orleans 2nd line) SLOW Track 56

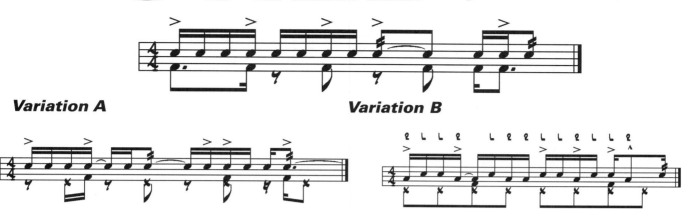

Variation A

Variation B

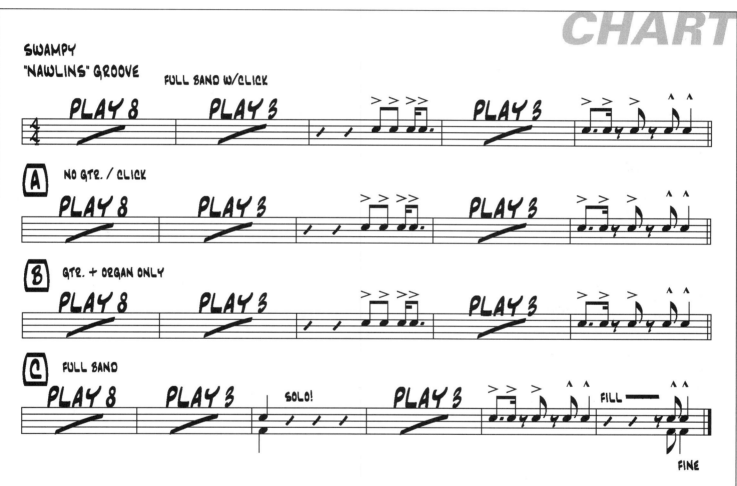

Revel in the loose swing of the band and how the feel stays round and syrupy. This is a New Orleans groove, so think gumbo!

Variation A has a little less bass drum activity, and Variation B features the floor tom getting in on the action. Watch that floor tom; it has a lot of power

WORLD

Groove 29 (New Orleans 2nd line) FAST Track 57

Notice the different rhythm in the first 2 bars and that this is our theme throughout the song. Watch your time on those drum breaks; there are a lot of them.

Both variations feature a little more rudimental spice. Variation A has a little flam mischief going on (which can be a groove enhancer or destroyer, depending on your flam control), and Variation B features a lot of roll work flowing through the groove.

Groove 30 Reggae SLOW Track 58

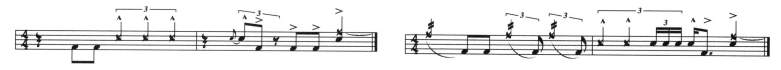

Variation A   **Variation B**

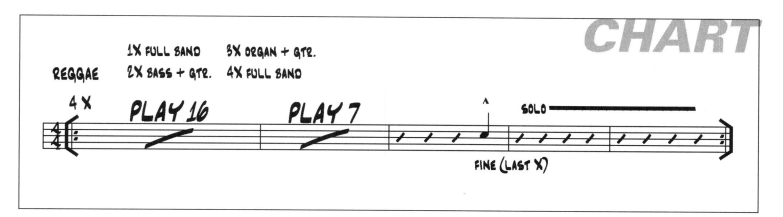

If there ever were two contradicting words in one sentence, they would be "reggae" and "chart." I'm willing to bet the chances of you seeing a chart on a real reggae gig are about as high as getting hit by lightning, but hey, it does happen.

Actually, speaking in terms of real life musical events, I'm presenting you with a chart, not because you would see a chart on a reggae gig, but because you might see a reggae chart on some *other* kind gig. For instance, you might find yourself playing a jingle, or a musical, or with a live band that switches grooves around; and you just need to know when and how long to play a reggae groove. Or, perhaps you've heard of gigs called "industrials." These are private gigs for companies or corporations; they are often elaborate mini-productions with dancers, lights, and a live band playing a variety of music of, well, you never know what.

Reggae is uniquely Jamaican and, as with many musical evolutions, it fused traits of African and European music with native Jamaican folk music; what was born and continues to this day is a music unique to the Jamaican culture. Interestingly, the music is increasingly popular today in hybrid styles that sometimes sound as much like real reggae as a polka (hey! Why isn't the polka in *Groove Essentials*? Next time . . .). Dance hall, reggaeton, and other rap/hip-hop/reggae fusions keep moving the music forward despite the usual resistance from the purists.

Reggae's golden era was in the 1970s when the music exploded globally. Of course, everyone has rightfully heard of the great Bob Marley, but there are many other artists worth hearing. Pick up a CD called *The Harder They Come* (it's also a movie); it's packed with artists and tracks that represent the classic reggae sound.

In *Groove Essentials* we will explore the classic "one drop" reggae beat, named as such because of its big lone bass drum note in each bar. To be sure, there are other ways to play reggae. Instead of beat variations, in Variations A and B, I give you some slick reggae fills to play at the ends of phrases or whenever a fill/solo seems appropriate.

WORLD

Groove 30 (Reggae) FAST Track 59

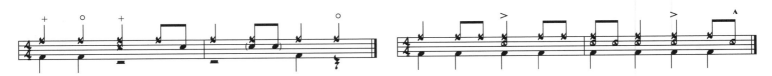

Variation A **Variation B**

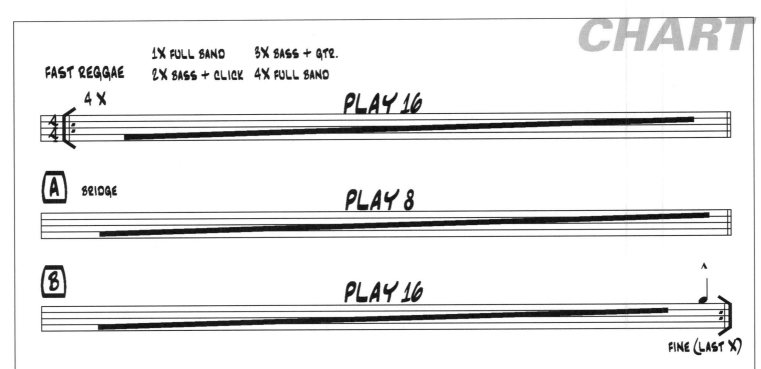

Our great bassist, Vashon Johnson, had a chance to unload on this track. The bass players in reggae music can be very virtuosic in their contribution to the groove, leaving the drums to anchor the bottom while the bass plays, interweaving lines that flow through the groove. In these situations, you really have to take care of business, and be the dependable rock so that the other musicians they can do their thing. You get a chance to focus on this when you play with the bass and click alone the second time through. Variations A and B represent different approaches to playing a reggae groove.

WORLD

Groove 31 CALYPSO Track 60

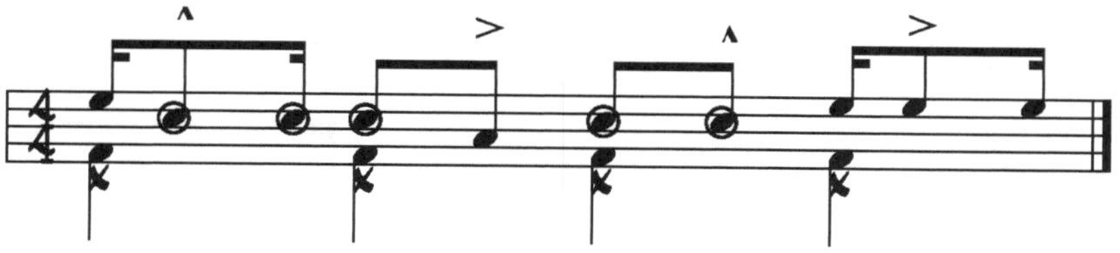

Variation A

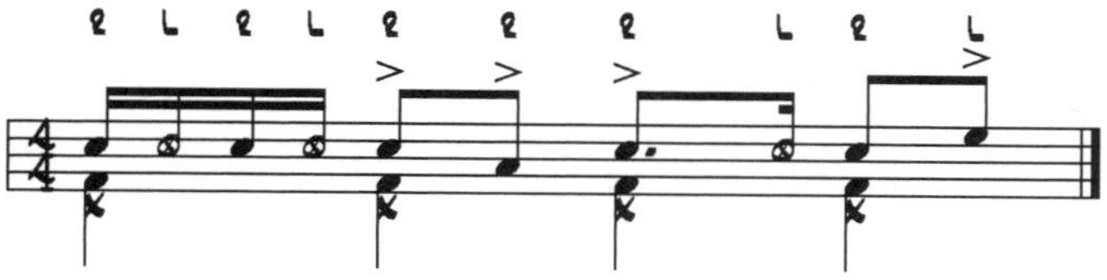

Variation B

CHART

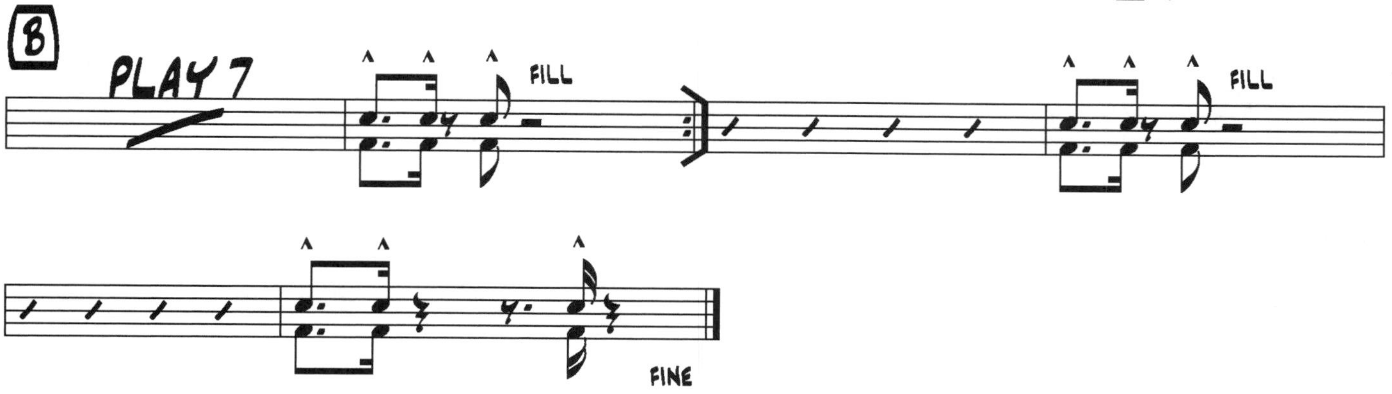

1X – FULL BAND   3X – NO BASS
2X – BASS + PERC.   4X – FULL BAND

CALYPSO

Another great groove from the Caribbean got its start in Trinidad: the calypso. Harry Belafonte recorded his famous "Banana Boat Song" ("Day-O!"), which brought the sound of calypso music into the mainstream. Steel drums (originally the tops of oil barrels) are a trademark calypso sound, and we'll hear them in this song.

Calypsos are fun to play because, as with most world beats, the drum part is quite active. Be careful to make your drumming clear and right in the pocket. You'll see on the DVD how to play this groove using your palm on the snare and a nice cross-stick sound. And please, don't forget to turn off your snares! If you don't, you'll sound like a marching band instead of a Caribbean rhythm section—hey, maybe that would sound cool, though.

Groove 32 SOCA Track 61

Variation A   **Variation B**

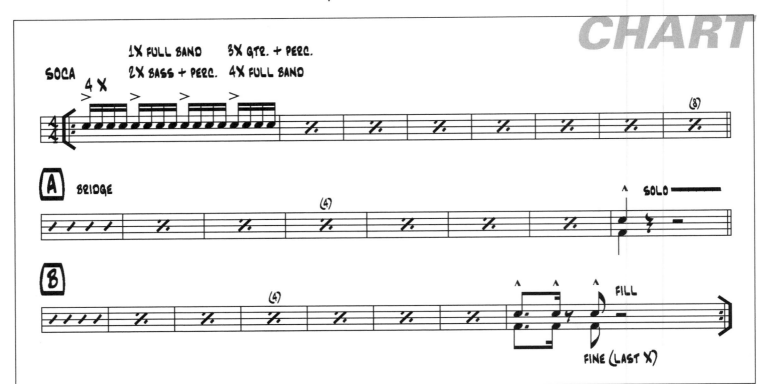

Depending on whom you believe, soca is a mix of calypso and Indian music, or soca is a hybrid groove combining elements of calypso and black soul music. Soul-Calypso ("So-Ca," get it?) is a very popular sound for percussionists, especially mallet players. I have yet to do a gig with a marimba player where at least part of the night wasn't devoted to Caribbean grooves, with soca being the main focus. I'm not complaining; on the contrary, I absolutely *love* playing these grooves. I think you will too.

The chart has an interesting way to write "time" in the first bar, wouldn't you say? If you see something like this or something similar to it, it's very unlikely that you would actually play what is written. Those sixteenth-notes are a composer's way of conveying the general "noteyness" of the groove, while relying upon you to know what a soca is and how to play it. The composer could be a trumpet player for all we know and probably can't write out a soca beat and why should s/he? We know how to play a soca, right? Well, let's see if we do . . .

Both variations have different characteristics to offer you. Variation A is less notey and a nice alternative to the basic groove, especially at faster tempos. Variation B has a slick 5-stroke roll that should be soft and exciting, rather than loud and flashy. Hey, you *are* recording yourself, of course, right?

Groove 33 BOSSA NOVA Track 62

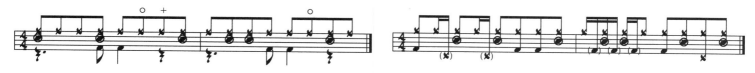

Variation A   **Variation B**

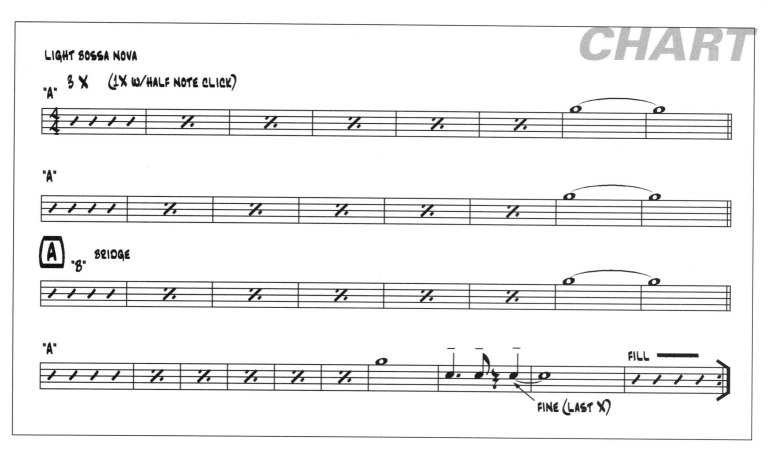

LIGHT BOSSA NOVA

"A" 3 X   (1X w/HALF NOTE CLICK)

"A"

[A] "B" BRIDGE

"A"

FINE (LAST X)

FILL

As we enter Brazil, please remember these grooves are so much more than the notes on the page. Brazilian music is a study within itself, and I can't get enough of it. As you play this gentle bossa nova ("the new beat" in Brazilian Portuguese), try to create something beautiful with your drums. Use a gentle touch and leave space while still creating the gorgeous feel of the bossa nova.

Variation A is a different approach with a leaner bass drum part and variation B should, honestly, have red warning flags around it. I'm showing you this variation only to demonstrate the possibility of implying a slight double-time feel inside a Bossa Nova and should be used with extreme sensitivity. But it sure sounds cool, though!

WORLD

Groove 34 SLOW SAMBA Track 63

Variation A

Variation B

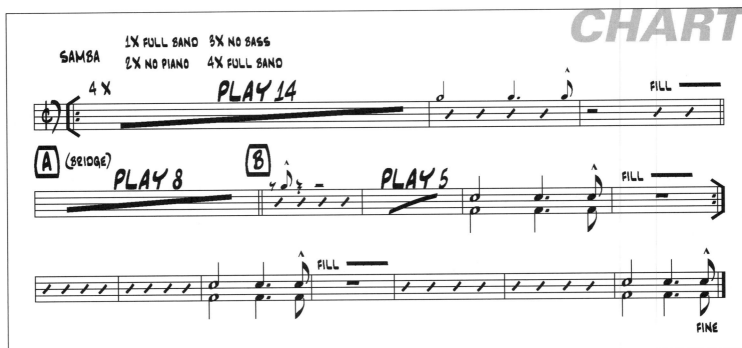

The samba is the classic sound of Brazil with a history as fascinating as any music style. Here, we have a great song to dig into and practice all that cool stuff I talk about on the DVD, such as making all the parts equal in volume and emulating the sound of a pandeiro (a large tambourine with a skin) on the hi-hat.

Listen, if you want to get the true feel of a samba, you have to let go of any notion you might have of playing "perfectly." The beauty of the samba is that it lies in that liquid state of straight *and* ever-so-slightly swung; it never settles into any one particular place. I studied with Portinho, my Brazilian drumset hero and master drummer, and even now, I still can't put his feel into words, so I won't try. Instead of trying to write the un-writeable, do what I did: Listen to the authentic music of the country and copy the feel of the masters. Then, see how you can apply their feel to *your* drumming.

Variations A and B are two different takes on playing this phenomenal music. Notice how the band is loose—not sloppy!—loose. There's a big difference.

Groove 34 MEDIUM SAMBA Track 64

Variation A   **Variation B**

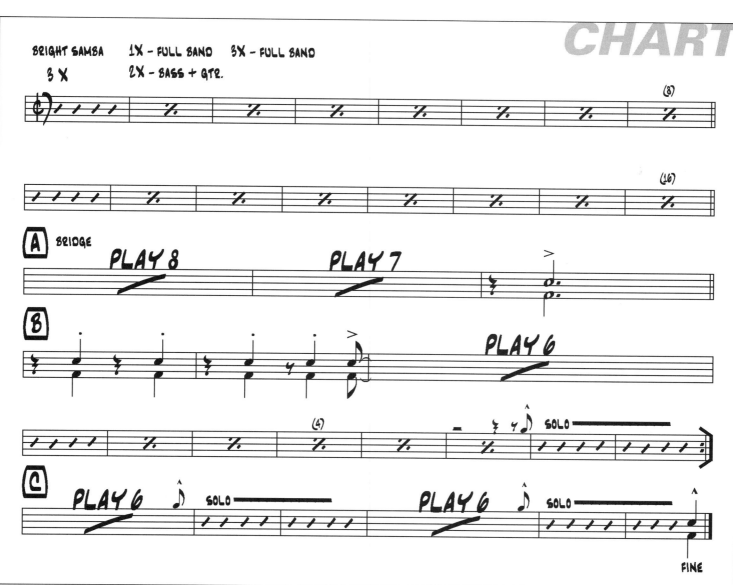

So, here lies the dichotomy: The tempo is medium, but the drums, since we're emulating the pandeiro on the hi-hat, are played very fast with the right hand. Obviously, part of this is a "chops" issue; if you can't play it fast, then you can't play it fast. However, if you desire to play it fast, then you must *practice* it fast, meaning that speed and staying relaxed is something that needs its own focus as does hand/foot independence, for example.

Look at yourself in the mirror when you try this groove. Are your shoulders up? Are you making horrible faces that convey pain and suffering? Don't just practice speed; practice *calm* speed. If you can't do it now, make yourself a chart and track your progress with the metronome, and please, take your time. It'll come . . .

WORLD

Groove 35 FAST SAMBA Track 65

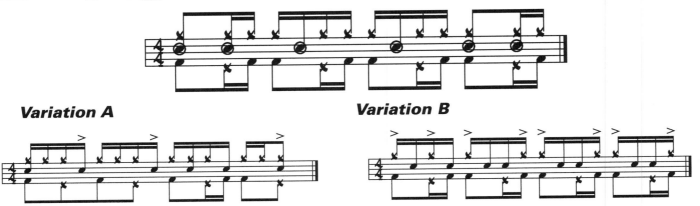

Variation A

Variation B

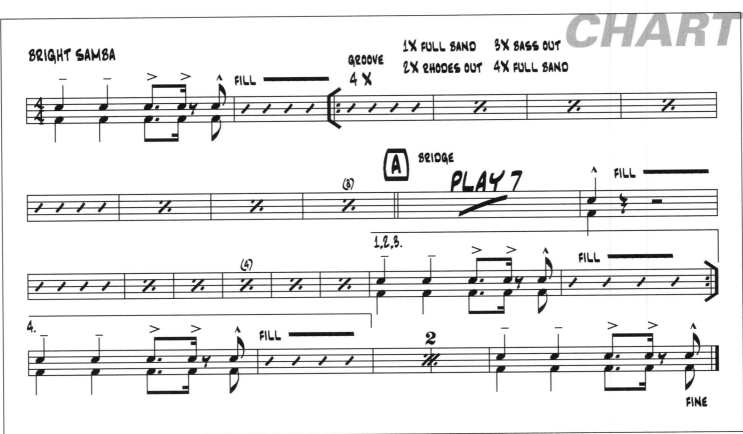

Ah . . . another dichotomy! Now we're playing fast, and it's actually easier to play than the medium-tempo samba we just played previously. Isn't music a strange beast? Keep your bass drum light and flowing forward. These fast sambas are very popular in jazz small groups; don't play too heavily or you'll stomp all over the other instruments. Light and crisp works every time.

Groove 36 BAIÃO SAMBA SLOW Track 66

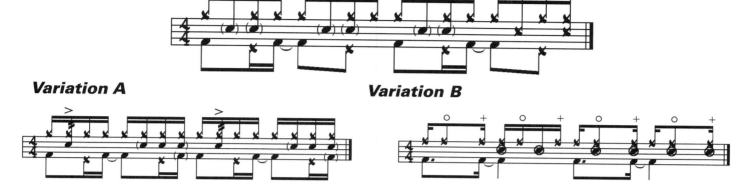

Variation A   **Variation B**

Here's another great groove from Brazil. How many great grooves can one place produce? We can't even get them all on the poster (*partido-alto* is another worth investigating). Look at the bass drum rhythm that the baião samba uses: the classic dotted eighth-sixteenth note. This rhythm and its 4/4 cousin, the dotted quarter-eighth, is one of the oldest rhythms known to music. It is also the basis for an entire groove and dance called the "Charleston." This rhythm was so ubiquitous that musicians from earlier generations actually refer to it exclusively as a "Charleston." When you listen to popular music now, you still hear it everywhere! It's the basis of many hip-hop and rap grooves, proving true the old adage that nothing's really new.

This rhythm is naturally syncopated in the bass drum so it has an entirely different feel and texture than the other Brazilian grooves we're exploring. On the DVD, I break this groove down so you can see how the parts work together to form the sound of the baião samba.

Variation A is another approach with some nice buzzes on the snare. Variation B is a very Brazilian approach to playing the hi-hat and is very, very tough to play well. However, if you can get it together, it sounds amazing.

WORLD

Groove 36 BAIÃO SAMBA FAST Track 67

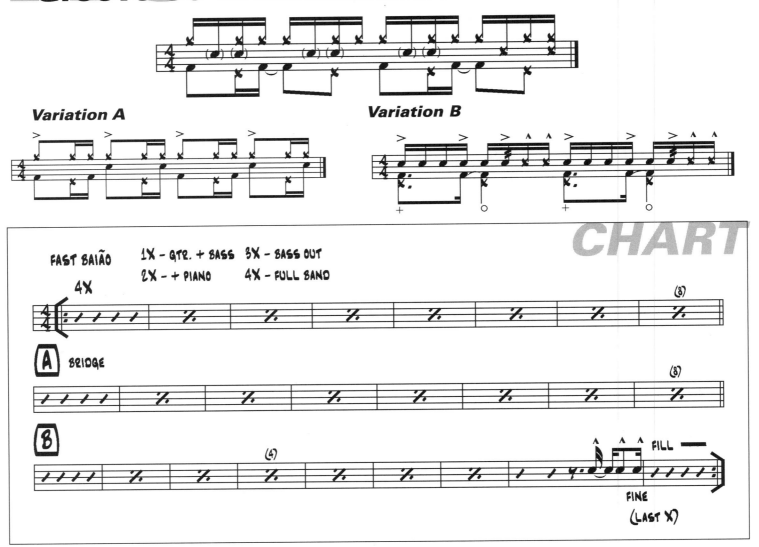

Variation A

Variation B

CHART

As usual, the faster the tempo gets, the louder you'll want to play. Avoid this natural phenomenon at all costs. Playing the drums harder will ruin this groove. Remember, we want to create a feeling of forward motion in the band, not weigh it down with clumsy drumming. When you listen to this track, you can hear how the entire band feels that syncopation of the baião samba and plays their parts accordingly. Help feed that syncopation to them, so they can do their thing on top of the groove.

Groove 37 BATUCADA SLOW Track 68

Variation A

Variation B

CHART

If there is a sound of Brazil and Carnival, it is the batucada. This is the groove that so many people associate with Brazil, sometimes more than the traditional sambas, such as Groove 34. However, it's important to remember that batucada is a samba, just another type.

The escolas de samba (samba schools) in Brazil are groups with thousands of participants, and many play the batucada. If you can't imagine what this sounds like, buy the Sergio Mendes CD, *Brasiliero.* Trust me; it's a sound like no other. This groove is, unlike the others grooves we've seen from Brazil, centered on the drums, with the snare being the main focus, and the floor tom simulating the surdo drum.

I recommend that you use the DVD and play along with me if you are having a tough time understanding how to play a batucada. It's a wonderful groove, but sometimes students have a hard time in the beginning knowing what exactly to play on the snare. It can turn into a rudimental cadence if you aren't careful. First of all, go for the overall flavor and feel of the groove rather than the exact notes. There is no perfect batucada part for the drumset; so, as always, we're going for the right *feel* more than trying to play a correct part. Variations A and B give you two wildly different versions to check out. Both work very well on this song, especially as an occasional spice.

Groove 37 BATUCUDA FAST Track 69

What am I going to say? What do I always say? Light and crisp when you play fast, right? And what else do I ask? Are you recording yourself? I knew you knew it. Variation A is a simple version of the batucada, and Variation B is a great fill measure to throw in once in awhile.

Groove 38 MERENGUE Track 70

Variation A

Variation B

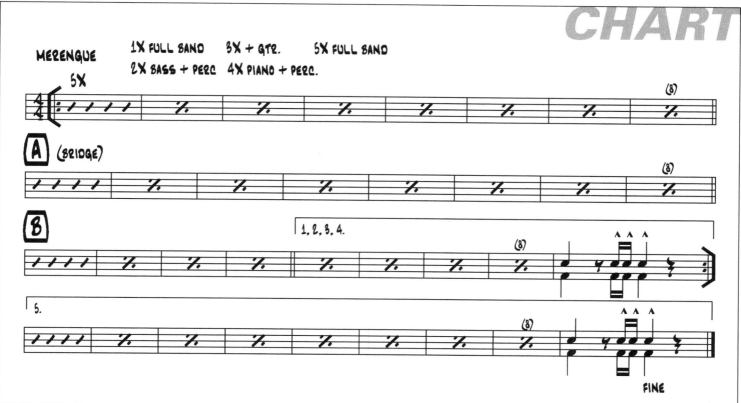

We've arrived at possibly the most energetic groove on the planet: the merengue—a groove with relentless forward motion like none other. I recommend that everyone, if possible, hear real Dominican bands play the merengue.

Once again, we're covering many percussion parts here, so if we were playing with a phalanx of percussionists on a gig, we would want to gently subtract from our contribution to avoid stepping on their parts. You can experiment with the parts each time through the song since each repeat is a little different. Listen to the incredible güiro playing of Rolando Morales-Matos that gives this merengue its authentic feel.

WORLD

Groove 39 CHA-CHA Track 71

Variation A

Variation B

First things first: *Groove Essentials* is not a primer on Afro-Cuban drumming. Specialized books are devoted to this deep subject. I recommend two in particular:

■ Frank Malabe's *Afro-Cuban Rhythms for Drumset* (MANHATTAN MUSIC/ALFRED PUBLICATIONS)

■ Tito Puente's *Drumming with the Mambo King* (HUDSON MUSIC)

These are necessary additions to any serious player's library and you can cop the grooves and concepts from the books and apply them to the songs in *Groove Essentials*.

To get started, we'll play a groove that everyone catches onto very quickly because of its relative simplicity, it's the cha-cha. Once again, as with all the examples that have only one tempo, the cha-cha lives in a relatively narrow tempo range compared to other grooves.

If you are playing with percussionists, Variation A might be a wise choice. Variation B simulates the sound of a güiro with the hi-hat, a little tricky to play, but well worth the effort.

The bolero, or the ballroom rhumba as its known in many circles, is a beautiful, romantic dance. So, think romance when you play it . . . elegant women in long gowns dancing with men in tuxedos who move proudly and with grace to the pulse of your beat. In other words, this ain't the chicken dance at Cousin Vinny's wedding—got it?

This a great song with a beautiful melody played on the guitar. Notice the little breaks at the ends of the phrases so the bass can play a short solo. Remember how in the beginning of the book we discussed how your fills and solos should sound related to the groove? Well, here is an example of a *bassist* filling perfectly when he has the opportunity. Drums aren't the only instrument that can fill, and we shouldn't play like they are. So, here we leave space for the bass to fill the hole and it works very nicely.

Variations A and B are both spices, not main grooves. Try each of them at the end of a phrase and see what you think.

Groove 41 MAMBO SLOW Track 73

Variation A   **Variation B**

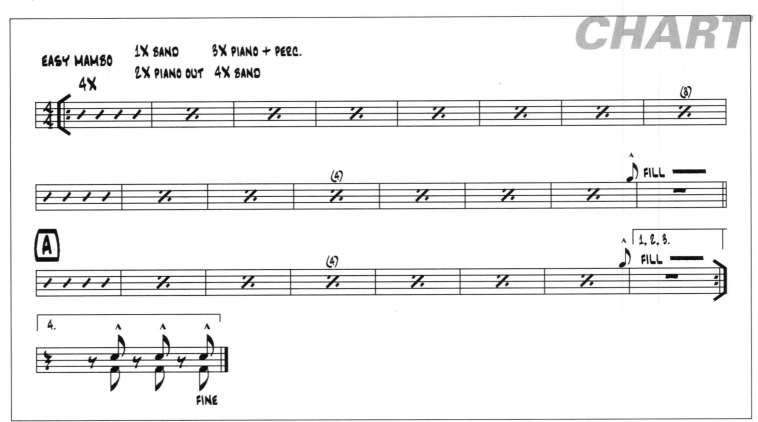

Some grooves that percussionists play in Afro-Cuban music transfer easily to the drumset, while some are a bit harder to adapt. The mambo is one of those grooves that sits on the drumset smooth as silk. It has a lot of parts going on, but for whatever reason, they just lock up and feel great on the drumset. Also, the mambo has a relatively large tempo range where it can live. We'll take a look at both ends of the spectrum.

The slow mambo is a great chance for you to get the parts working in a tempo that isn't too crazy. Once you get the basics out of the way, try to focus on the music and how all your parts fit with the percussion, bass, and piano. You'll notice how much more rhythmically dense these grooves are compared to the rock section; for that reason, you have to bring a higher sense of rhythmic sensitivity to your drumming. Try to think in terms of creating *one* sound, instead of playing many parts.

Variation A has a triplet in the second bar, which is nice to throw to throw in occasionally as a spice. Variation B is great to play with a multitude of percussionists and keeps the music less cluttered.

Groove 41 MAMBO FAST Track 74

Variation A

Variation B

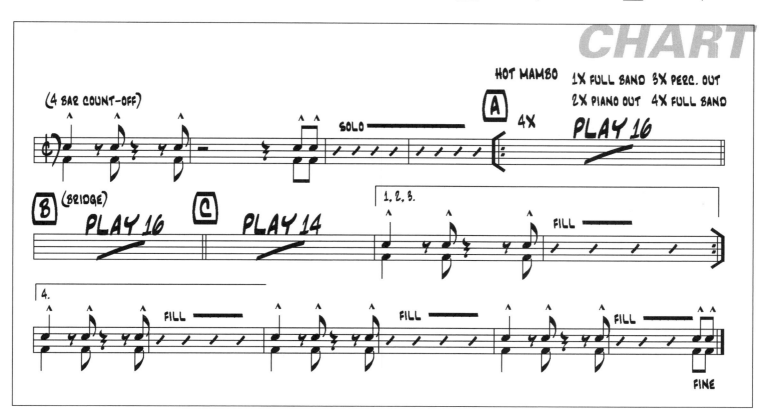

There is an ensemble figure in this chart that happens again and again in this tune. Take a look at it now; it's right there in the very first bar. See it? Be afraid. Be very afraid. It looks so cute and innocent doesn't it? Well it's not. It's an evil little rhythm. I don't know what it is, but it's tricky to get everyone to play this figure the same way. Fortunately, since the band on the track is tight, you'll get to see if *you* have command of that figure. Here's a hint: Don't rush the last note.

This is the kind of track that you can really dig into and have great time as it just cooks from the first note and doesn't stop. As the instrumentation changes on each repeat, take the time to analyze the groove choices you are making such as volume and adding or subtracting parts. It's so easy to be in your own world and play self-serving fills and grooves. I'm asking you to record yourself (Hey! It's been too long . . .) and listen impartially to your performance. It's hard to do, but it's great for your playing. Now, go mambo to your heart's content.

Oh, Variations A and B are both good alternatives when playing with percussionists (depending on what parts *they* are playing, course).

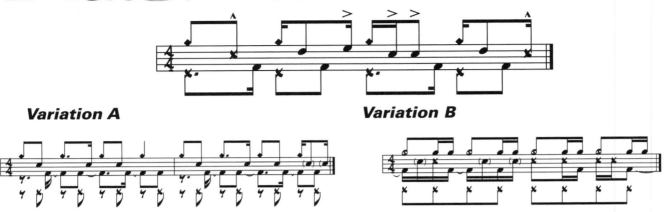

Variation A   **Variation B**

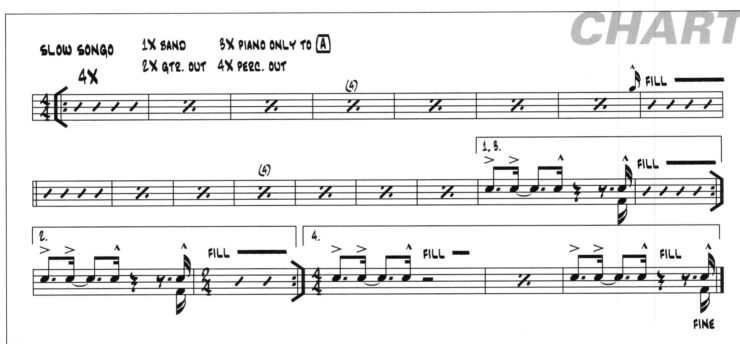

Hallelujah! An Afro-Cuban groove actually created for the drumset! Until now, we've been borrowing parts from the percussionists and applying them to the drumset; now, we have something to call our own. Please don't use the songo as a blanket groove for everything that even remotely sounds Latin. The songo is a great groove, but doesn't fit everywhere.

Look at the figure in the very last bar of the chart. Look familiar? It should, because it's the same scary figure we just saw and discussed in "Groove 41 Fast," only this time it's written in 4/4 instead of 2/2 (cut-time). Another shared trait from the previous chart is that we stop clean many times on the last sixteenth-note of a bar, such as the next-to-last bar on the first line. This is a signature sound of Latin and much sixteenth-note based music. It's critical you play this important rhythmic feature with control, and without losing the time or the groove.

Variation A is an example of a songo with less inner motion on the toms than the main groove. Variation B is a completely different approach that is tough to play but sounds wonderful when played well.

Groove 42 SONGO FAST Track 76

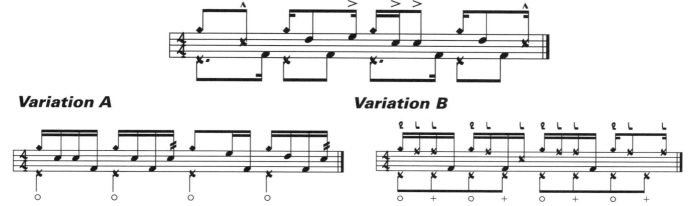

Variation A

Variation B

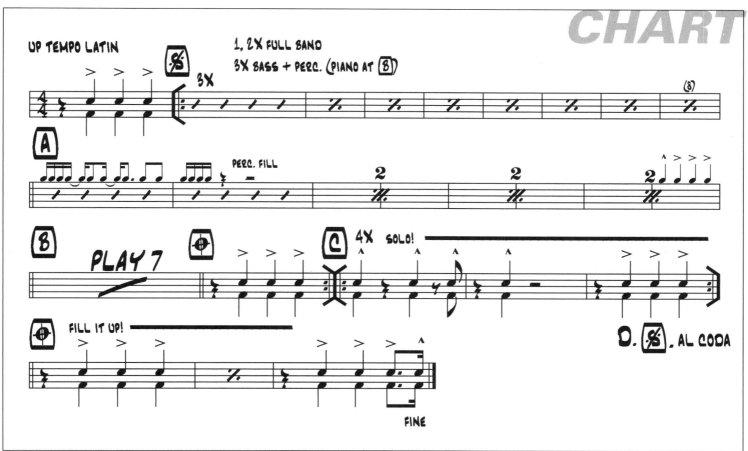

Here's our first D.S. al Coda—a special moment for those of you just discovering the joys of chart reading. So here's what you do: At the end of Letter C, go back to the sign (𝄋), play all the way to the bar before Letter C, and then jump to the Coda (⊕) for the last 3 bars.

There is solo space in this chart as well as an ensemble riff at Letter A, so there's enough going on to keep you busy for quite awhile. If you don't want to solo, then don't; simply practice your songo through the solo section. Everyone will enjoy locking into the amazing lightning-fast conga work of Mr. Morales-Matos.

Groove 43 NAÑIGO SLOW Track 77

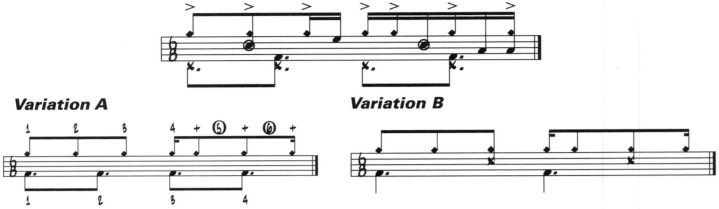

Variation A

Variation B

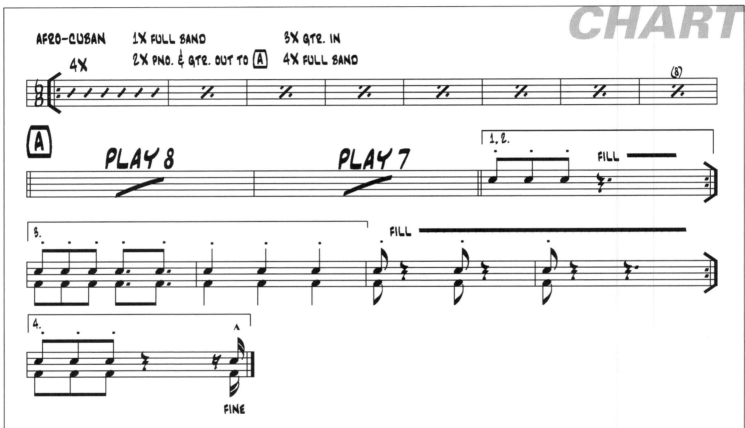

CHART

The nañigo can really throw drummers a curve the first time they try to play it. To help, Variation A has the "six" over "four" counting spelled out for you (refer to the DVD if your head is spinning right now); and Variation B is a very simple way to play this groove as an alternative to the main groove, which can prove to be a bit of a challenge.

I've kept the click in softly for you (you've probably noticed I've left it in for the first time through on many of the world grooves), so you can get your bearings and hear how the band relates to the click. Once you get the hang of thinking in "six," you'll be fine. Also check out the unexpected ensemble rhythms in the third ending, giving more advanced players a chance to wind their way through some interesting figures.

Groove 43 NAÑIGO FAST Track 78

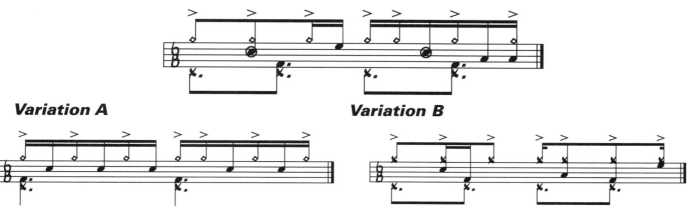

Variation A   **Variation B**

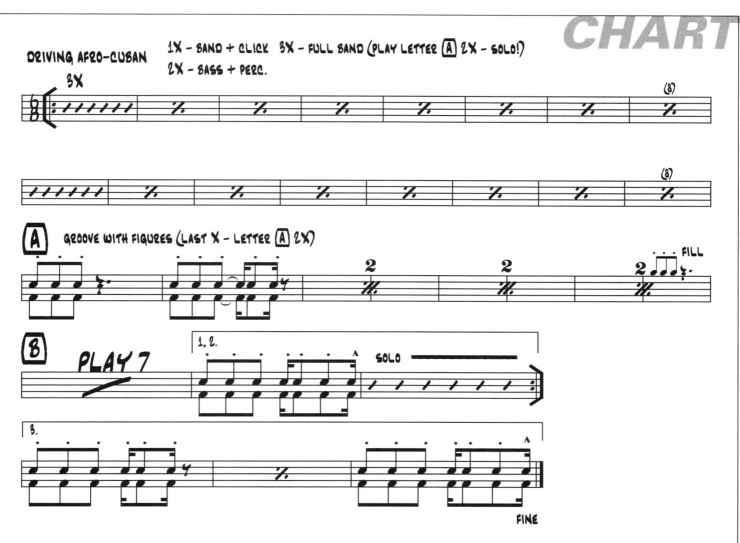

One of the more advanced charts in *Groove Essentials* is presented here. You can groove through Letter A, but advanced players may like to solo over the figures. To help beginners, the first time through the form, you'll hear the "six" click in the left ear and the "four" click in the right.

Groove 44 MOZAMBIQUE Track 79

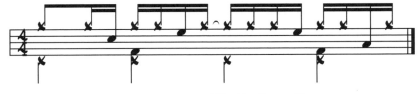

Variation A   **Variation B**

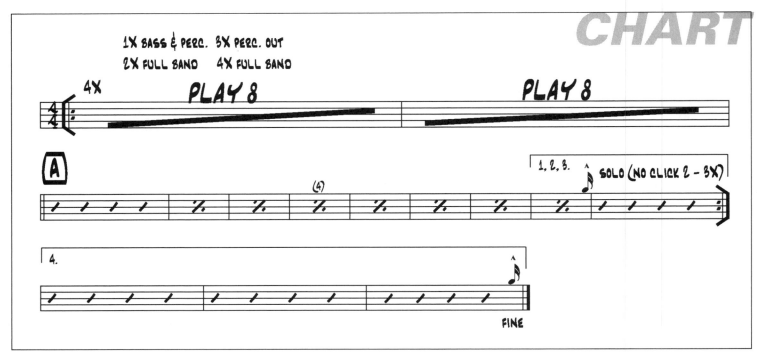

This mozambique groove was thrust into the spotlight when Steve Gadd used it on the Paul Simon song "Late in the Evening." After that, everybody had to learn a mozambique.

The signature bell pattern of the mozambique should be your focus. The underpinning tom interplay is sometimes confusing (again, notice the rhythmic density of the world grooves), and if so, just play the bell pattern. You'll notice on the DVD that I cross hands to play the floor tom with my left stick. This is comfortable for me, but for many drummers it's not; so if you are one who gets stuck in the choreography of the crossing motion, then simply play the tom part on the upper toms. It works just fine there too.

Both Variations A and B have something unique to offer: Variation A has the bass drum on all the downbeats, and Variation B has the hi-hat playing the active eighth notes with the foot and the bass drum taking over the rhythm of the toms.

Groove 45 SALSA Track 80

Variation A

Variation B

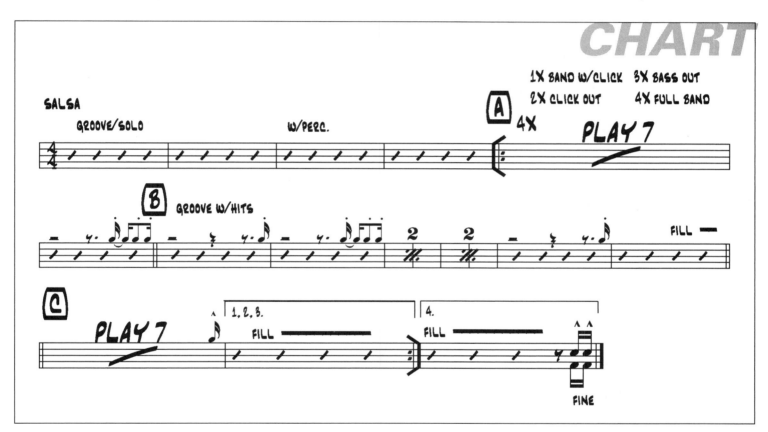

"Salsa"—a term many master Latin musicians hate! Tito Puente legendarily despised the term "salsa," insisting on calling his music the correct term for whatever he was playing, such as "cha-cha" or "mambo." But, like technology, it's silly to resist the march of progress even when it's not necessarily progressive. "Salsa" is a term that is here to stay. So, let's salsa . . .

Here we have the clave rhythm in the left hand playing the cross stick sound, while the right hand plays the traditional cáscara (shell) rhythm on the cowbell. Once again, understanding clave, specifically the difference between son and rumba clave, and the phrasing (3:2 or 2:3), and how these things affect not only you but the entire ensemble, is essential for authentic playing. So, buy those books and enjoy the journey.

I've yet to play a salsa gig by myself; there is always percussion in the band. So, Variation A is a great thing to play to just stay out of the way if you have five hand drummers all fighting for space. You don't want to get in the middle of that, trust me. Variation B is a backwards phrasing of the main groove so you can see what it sounds like with a different twist.

Groove 46 TANGO Track 81

Variation A

Variation B

CHART

Listen closely: If you play the tango like a dead fish, some crazed Argentinean will find you and set fire to your drumset. Don't laugh, I've heard stories . . .

You'll have a great time with this chart; it has a lot of space for some snare drum soloing. Take it easy on the rudiments and play tango-esque ideas.

Groove 47 BEGUINE Track 82

Variation A

Variation B

CHART

BEGUINE   1X FULL BAND   3X NO PERC.
4X   2X NO PIANO   4X FULL BAND

SOLO _____

A

(8)

(12)

B (LAST X - PIANO SOLO) -

(8)

FINE

The gorgeous beguine finishes out this world section. It's a beautiful groove from Martinique that you'll find popping up in organized situations such as Broadway musicals. Enjoy this track and the beautiful sweeping feel created by the entire band. Variation A has a harder accent on the "and of 1," a sound that many prefer in a beguine. Variation B uses a little snare roll to help move things along.

WORLD

World Groove Music Starter

Boldly I go, sure to infuriate every even semi-knowledgeable lover of a genre, because I didn't include Artist X. Well, take it easy—the guys below are pretty good too.

BRAZILIAN

Caetano Veloso
Sergio Mendes
Gilberto Gil
Djavan
Manfredo Fest
Daniela Mercury
Antonio Carlos Jobim
Timbalada
Carlinhos Brown
Olodum
Ivan Lins

AFRO-CUBAN/LATIN (various styles)

Irakere
Paquito D'Rivera
Arturo Sanduval
Buena Vista Social Club
Cachao
Tito Puente
Chico O'Farrill
Eddie Palmieri
Pancho Sanchez
Cubanismo
Michel Camilo
Gonzalo Rubalcaba
Danilo Perez
Snowboy and the Latin Section
Francisco Aguabella
Viva Cubop (great Latin-Jazz compilations)
Mongo Santamaria

DOMINICAN MERENGUE

Juan Luis Guerra
Sergio Vargas
Jossie Esteban
Los Hermanos Rosario

REGGAE

Bob Marley
Jimmy Cliff
Dennis Brown
The Maytals
Don Drummond

NEW ORLEANS 2ND LINE and More

Just remember that 2nd Line is a groove, not really a sub-genre of New Orleans music in and of itself, so familiarize yourself with these terms: Zydeco, Cajun, Swamp, Funk, Rag, Blues, Gospel, Roots, and Brass Bands. In any of those situations, they may whip out a 2nd-line groove. Ya never know.

Professor Longhair
Dr. John
Dirty Dozen Brass Band
Jon Cleary
The Neville Brothers
The Meters
Buckwheat Zydeco
Lafayette Rhythm Devils

TANGO

The recording *Tango Argentino: Traditional & Modern* has some of the classic lo-fi and very raw recordings that true tango lovers enjoy, but it also has some more modern recording where you can actually hear the drums.

CALYPSO and SOCA

To people unfamiliar with this music, I always recommend two recordings:

- **Steelbands of Trinidad & Tobago**
- **Steel Band Music of the Caribbean**

Both are very lo-fi compilations but are authentic examples of the real grooves.

BEGUINE

Check out *Asi Es el Beguine* to hear the real thing. To hear this groove applied to a musical, listen to the legendary *West Side Story*.

GLOBAL TOURS

Chapter 6
GLOBAL TOURS

Okay, here's where it all comes together. The final goal for any true professional musician is to flow from style to style with grace, artistry, and command without you or your audience thinking in such classroom terms as "genre" and "groove parts." Nobody cares at all about that stuff when it's time to make music. To be sure, you must do the hard work to understand and execute what you need to play, but at some point, it has to be about making music, and especially, making the music feel great, because, at the end of the day, that is what we as drummers do. These 15-minute extravaganzas are designed to help you achieve that lofty goal.

Each of the three global tours makes five stops, and all three are constructed to give you different challenges. Stop now if you haven't tried all the grooves in the book separately first. The idea is that you have some command of all the grooves by themselves before you tackle these beasts.

Global Tour #1

Let's see where we're going in "Global Tour #1":

- **Fast Rock**

- **Slow Shuffle**

- **Calypso**

- **Slow Funk**

- **Fast Baião**

The first thing you'll notice is that, as usual, the drums are the conduit to all things that segue musically (blend seamlessly). The drums set up the shuffle into Letter A; the drums set up the slow funk into Letter C; the drums set up the fast samba at Letter D. Man, they work us like dogs. The only segue that does not rely on the drums is the one into Letter B, where the whole band shifts into a bright calypso.

Remember my advice on fills/solos; it applies here more than ever: Your fills and solos should sound related to the groove. Only now, your segue fills will sound related to the groove you are *introducing*, not the groove you are leaving behind.

Again, I'd like to stress that this book is designed for you to fail the first time you try. The charts are underwritten; they intentionally don't tell you things you'd like to know. The music has no click; heck, it doesn't even have percussion on most of it. Now I'm throwing you into a very professional situation with no rehearsal and expecting you to sink or swim. So, perhaps you'll sink. So what? Sink a little less the next time, and the next, and next, and before you know it, you'll be global touring your butt off. Good luck! Have fun with these!

GLOBAL TOURS

Global Tour #2

- ■ Fast Swing

- ■ Slow Rock

- ■ Fast New Orleans-2nd Line

- ■ Slow Songo

- ■ Merengue (Fast, of course!)

This global tour features some very dramatic segues with severe tempo shifts. Be ready for them! In this entire book, I never provide you with tempo markings such as quarter note=138 bpm. You won't see them in professional charts. If you want to know the tempos, a good drill is to use your metronome, discover the numerical value and then write it in yourself. That's what I do on gigs when I want to know the tempos, because I know they aren't going to be written in for me. Unless the music is on a click track, the conductor or the music director will not want to be locked into a specific metronome marking because "fast" one night may not be "fast enough" the next night. So, try not to be rigid in your thinking of tempos; you may be called upon to adjust them in real life.

That's the beautiful thing when you start to become "trusted" by the leader of a band; s/he will let you put the tempo where it feels good, which is always better than shooting for a number on a metronome any day. So, off you go on "Global Tour #2"; send me a postcard or something.

GLOBAL TOURS

Global Tour #3

The last of our global tours is the most challenging and the most athletic in terms of sheer energy; you'll get a good workout with this one. What's on the menu? Glad you asked:

- **Cha-Cha**

- **Fast R&B (Funky-Swing-Thing-That-Really-Defies-a-Category Groove)**

- **Fast Jazz Waltz in "1"**

- **Slow Bossa Nova**

- **Fast Mambo**

This global tour not only has severe segues; it also has drastically unrelated grooves mashing into each other. That's what makes it so much fun—a swing/funk thing morphing into a fast jazz waltz? Love it! To top it off, for advanced players, there is a lot of solo space too.

Interesting story—you know, there used to be things on television called "variety shows" that, as their name implies, had a lot of variety. You'd see a singer, then a juggler, then a comic, then a vocal group, then a dancer, and on and on for an hour. They've since fallen out of favor for superior entertainment like *Baywatch*. My father, Sonny Igoe, was the drummer for the CBS and NBC orchestras when they had such things; he showed me a few of the charts that they would play for these variety shows. They were impossibly long charts; 10–15 pages were not uncommon, and they flowed all the over the place rhythmically and stylistically. That's hard enough to do, but they were doing it all live on television. Isn't that amazing to think of now in our sterile shiny digital world? No second chances, no fixing in the mix; it was live to millions of people right then and there. That, my friends, is pressure. And to top it off, every week they had a new big pile of charts to plow through, live, on the air. The closest things to something like that now are the Letterman/Leno shows or *Saturday Night Live*. However, those shows have a fraction of a fraction of the music that variety shows had to navigate, not to mention that the network orchestras of yesteryear were full orchestras, complete with strings. If you're lucky, you can catch some of these variety shows on classic TV stations. If you do, just think about the fact that not only were these guys sight-reading practically everything you're hearing, but they are also playing it live on the air. When you play the global tours, it's fun to think of yourself in that kind of situation and imagine having to nail it the first time.

ENDURE Track 86

The last tune on the DVD is a piece entitled "Endure." Since I play it on the DVD, I'm offering it to you here, but let it be known that this is a very challenging piece of music that requires the conceptualization of many advanced topics. I started out writing this composition as a tribute to one of my favorite artists, the Senegalese singer Youssou N'Dour ("Endure"—get it?), but as usually happens with my pieces, all sorts of other influences came to the party. You can hear harmonic ideas from the Yellowjackets and rhythmic mischief à la Chick Corea. However, at its core, the idea was to explore, as N'Dour does, the line between playing in "6," "4," and "3," and blurring the lines between them.

The three grooves explored in "Endure" are:

■ **6/8 Afro-Cuban (heavily modified to our musical needs)**

■ **Half-Time Shuffle**

■ **Funk in 3/4 time (soloing over it)**

The long solo breaks are something you'll want to practice over and over again, and I'm leaving the click in for you here. After you get comfortable, please don't be a slave to the click and play stiff, "vertical" solo ideas. Rather, think of the click as a very reliable dance partner that you know can take care of itself if you decide to go off on your own for a second or two. Thinking in this way will allow you to play longer, "linear" solo ideas that flow forward and keep the listener's ear intrigued.

The take you see on the DVD was my one and only shot to get this, because literally, there was an unbelievable blizzard raging outside (January of 2004), and everyone in the production crew had to pack up and try to get back to Brooklyn or risk being stranded for two days in the woods of upstate New York. So, you can see what I mean about pressure: sometimes it brings out the best you have.

EXTRA! EXTRA! EXTRA!
EXTRA Listening, EXTRA Practice EXTRA Tracks

As exhaustive as *Groove Essentials* is, there are, of course, other great grooves that didn't make the book, poster or DVD. Even though my first draft for the poster contained over 120 grooves, it was never the goal of *Groove Essentials* to contain every single groove ever created (a fool's quest, for sure). Rather, the idea was to expose the student to the main groove families and supply a strong foundation for individual exploration of the grooves you may run across.

For example, drum & bass (or Jungle) grooves are very popular with drummers because of the slick sound of those Funk beats sped up like they are in that genre. Hey, Funk grooves! You've got three of them in your hands right now. See? You can apply the concepts of those grooves, if not the exact grooves note for note, to any style that may come your way. Discovering any commonality between groove genres, rather than trying to segregate them into brick-walled categories is always recommended.

The disc includes two bonus tracks for your listening/practicing pleasure:

■ Track 87/"Chart Talkdown"—Books are great, but there is nothing like hearing a teacher explain something as it's actually happening. So, here's your chance to have me gabbing in your ear for a blow-by-blow description on how to read a chart, just like a private lesson. If you are new to reading, or have never seen a chart before, this would be a great place to start your *Groove Essentials* experience.

■ Track 88/"The 21-Minute Jazz Ramp"- This is a something I give my more advanced students so they can feel how swing changes (gradually straightens) as it gets faster. It also allows them to analyze how they function at all ranges of tempo from slow to very fast. Every two chorus' gets bumped up by about 10 bpm. You will learn a lot about your swing feel when playing "The 21-Minute Jazz Ramp". Put a timer next to your drums and glance up every once in a while. Match the time with the tempos below and you'll get an idea of where you are on the metronome. The idea isn't just to survive the "Jazz Ramp" without your right hand falling off, but to function smoothly and musically across the entire tempo range. Remember, the lower end of the ramp needs as much attention, if not more, than the upper end. Good luck and have fun!

   Start 75 bpm
   5 minutes 105 bpm
   10 minutes 145 bpm
   12 minutes 175 bpm
   14 minutes 205 bpm
   16 minutes 260 bpm
   18 minutes 300 bpm
   20 minutes (last 2 chorus') 350 bpm.

About the Disc

The included disc contains all the tracks in MP3 format. To fit this much material on regular audio CDs would require five discs and a much higher $$ in that box on the back cover. For my fellow geeks, you might find it interesting that the disc is encoded at the highest possible quality from 192K–320K using Logic Pro 7, so there will be no audible loss of resolution from the original source material.

As a convenience, each MP3 file is encoded with the "Artist" category as "Tommy Igoe" and the "Album" category as "Groove Essentials" so on a computer, the files will organize themselves however you wish. Also, each file has the tempo (Beats Per Minute or bpm) of the song included as well. So, in iTunes, your viewing options are plentiful.

An interesting fact about MP3 discs is that they are really data discs, so we had to trick the disc into listing the tracks in the correct order by using two dummy letters in front of every track title. Remember, each MP3 title on the disc contains the groove number and tempo. For example, "aa 1-slow.mp3" on your disc is "Groove 1 Slow" in the book. If you are dumping the tracks into your computer, you can delete the first two letters of each track if you wish.

Here are some ways you can play the disc:

1. **If you have an MP3-capable CD or DVD player, simply pop in the disc, and the tracks will come up just as with a regular audio CD.**

2. **Even the cheapest, most basic modern computer comes with a CD/DVD drive with audio capability and the software needed to play the tracks. iTunes® software is free and available for Windows and Macintosh at www.apple.com. There are scores of other MP3 programs available as well.**

3. **Via your computer, you can dump these songs into your iPod® or any other portable MP3 player. iPods are great to practice with, because it's easy to manipulate the track's position, as opposed to regular CD players.**

If you don't have an MP3-capable disc player, you can convert the tracks into regular audio discs that play in all CD players in just about any computer using any number of free software options. Simply transfer all the tracks onto your hard drive, and then burn them onto discs in "CD Audio" format. Be aware that the audio quality goes down when you change formats, so to hear everything in its natural pristine state, stay with MP3s.

Even if you don't own any of the mentioned items, you still have options. Your local library probably has the necessary computers and help needed to transfer the tracks onto audio CDs. Just bring blank CDs with you. Perhaps a free night-computer course at your local school or community center might do the trick, or a friend with a computer could help you out.

But if you are a stickler for quality like I am, at the very least you'll want to pick up an MP3-capable CD or DVD player. At the time of this writing, portable MP3-capable CD players are available for less than 15 bucks! The convenience and advantage of having all the tracks on one disc and at full audio quality cannot be overstated. Even though there is a lot of button pressing to get to, say, Track 63; it's much more convenient than actually stopping the disc, popping out Disc #2, changing to Disc #4—or wait was it Disc #3?—and then pressing more buttons again. Of course, an iPod is easiest of all; just spin your thumb, hit the button, and you're at Track 88.

After the music fades...

Tell me, did you have fun? I hope so because like I've always said, if you can't have fun playing the drums, then… well, I don't know, but you should definitely have fun playing the drums, don't you think? I'd like to congratulate you on whatever you've experienced in Groove Essentials. Whether you felt success, failure, curiosity, anger, pride, frustration—whatever—I'm sure they were real emotions you experienced while playing this music; for me, that's what it's all about. I said before that this book was designed for you to fail, and I mean that in the kindest of ways. A book you succeed at the first time is worthless while the book that challenges you and taunts you, just daring you to come back for one more try is worth its weight in gold. A good music book is a friendly sparring partner, and I hope I've created a worthy adversary for you.

It's time I let you in on why I wrote Groove Essentials, and why I've poured my heart and soul into this project. It isn't to get rich (rich from a drum book, that's funny!), or gain publicity and notoriety. It's because, from where I sit in the world of drumming education, there's a need for Groove Essentials. You won't find licks or twirls, or double bass or one-handed rolls, or James Brown grooves sped up to hypersonic speeds. You won't find out how to play 11 with your right hand, 5 with your left hand while mopping the floor with your left foot and simultaneously singing ancient Gregorian chant. You won't find every possible mathematical permutation of a rock beat on one page followed by even more pages of mangled/hybrid/convoluted/shifted-until-they-scream-for-mercy beats on another. Not that there is anything wrong with those things, but you would never play them in a real band on a real gig with real musicians and, if you did, you'd be shown the door, probably with a foot to your posterior to make the point perfectly clear.

I'm a practical kind of guy, that's just my nature and it carries over into my education philosophy. With all the diverse options available in books, DVD's and the Internet, the young drummer (and not-so-young, too!) has to be careful on the advice s/he absorbs. As with anything, it's a challenge to sift through the static to get to the music. When I see a kid at a music store buy a copy of "SLAUGHTER-SPEED BASS DRUM TECHNIQUE GUARANTEED TO THRASH ALL THOSE WHO DARE STAND NEAR!" it's all I can do to not rip the box from his hands and run out the door cackling like some crazed revivalist, "Another Saved! Another Saved!"

As a player/teacher who enjoys existing equally on both levels, I'm often sought out to help drummers who, in their frustration, just can't seem to play music very well. Sure, they can play sixteenths with one foot and a click at 200 bpm, but can they play in a band? No pocket, no groove confidence, no nothing. What's the problem? Bad advice, pure and simple. For example, if you spend a lot of time trying to play rolls with your feet, then you've got a problem—unless the one goal in your drumming life is to play with the three existing speed-metal bands that would actually need you to do that. You can practice it if you want to; I practice bizarre stuff too just for fun, because it is fun! But as a ratio of your practice day, it had better be what it needs to be. Bizarre stuff is the icing—groove is the cake. And nobody eats icing without cake, except my son, but he's two years old.

Regardless of where you want to go with your drumming, you can be sure that playing with other musicians and having musical worth yourself, will be required of you if you want to drum outside your practice room. With the global landscape of music fusing at an ever-expanding pace, the versatile drummer— the drummer who understands what groove, time and feel mean to the entire band, not just the drums— owns the advantage. And that . . . is why Groove Essentials was created.

I'd like to thank the academy...

I'm big on thanking the people who help make things possible, so let me get this out of my system. One person doesn't produce a project of this scope by himself; I needed a lot of help to transform *Groove Essentials* from an idea into an actual book. Huge thanks to Jo Hay, graphic designer; Gayle Giese, text editor; and Jack Mansager, notation engraver; each of whom have been incredibly supportive and generous in lending their talents to this book. Gayle is going to read something very minimalist after all the pruning she had to do from my original text.

The musicians, it goes without saying, can't be recognized or thanked enough: Kevin Kuhn, guitar; Ted Baker, keyboards; Allen Farnham, keyboards; Vashon Johnson, basses; Rolando Morales-Matos, percussion; and Darmon Meader, saxophones ("Endure"). I don't need to go on and on about the amazing talent of these guys; after all, you've been playing with them for a while yourself. No words suffice to convey my appreciation; I can't imagine even *trying* to produce this project without them by my side.

Of course, the publishers and my friends, Rob Wallis and Paul Siegel of Hudson Music need to be thanked as well. Listen, I'm an opinionated pain-in-the-butt about the stuff I create, and I need the freedom to toil away like a mad scientist with a Do-Not-Disturb sign on the door without anyone bothering me. Our relationship has reached that level of mutual respect. They patiently wait for me to finish, hoping—with eyes closed and fingers crossed—that the final product doesn't have 530 pages, 17 DVDs and a free pony.

Thanks go to my music proofreaders, Wayne Dunton, Brendan Buckley and Carter McLean who went through the book and found, oh I don't know, about 500 errors or so. Squashed 'em all like bugs they did. Really, can you imagine proofing this whole book for notation errors? I can't and I wrote it!

Other people who helped with advice, support or inspiration in one form or another are Sonny Igoe, Rick Drumm, Vic Firth, The Zildjian Family, John DeChristopher, John Wittman, James Genus, Dennis Delucia, Larry Cohen, Clint de Ganon, Portinho, Lew Anderson, Darmon Meader, Karl Jurman, Joe Church, Horacio Hernandez, Vinnie Colaiuta, Steve Gadd, Carlinhos Brown, Elvin Jones, and Buddy Rich. Also, thanks to all the students who, over the last 20 years or so, have helped make me the educator I am today. I've learned as much from all of you as you have from me, if not more. Now, where's my money?! (My private students are laughing right now, trust me.)

If you don't mind bearing with me for just one more paragraph, I have to thank my incredible family including my amazing wife, Jessica. Listen, as we got close to deadline on this thing, I basically didn't see her for the last four weeks—she didn't make a peep—and we have 18-month-old twins! Now that, ladies and gentlemen, is a supportive wife. My babies, Sofia and Jordan, get big thanks too for being the best, easiest babies in the world. Of course I thank my amazing parents, Sonny and Claire Igoe, and my in-laws Diane and Bill Benwell, Jack, Erica, John and Elizabeth Bryndza and Linda Rocco, as well as the rest of my family and friends that I would list, but I'm out of room and everybody's tired. It's a long book after all . . .

I'd love to hear how everyone makes out with the book and music. I'll be posting comments from users of *Groove Essentials/The Play-Along* on my website (www.tommyigoe.com), so shoot me an e-mail when you can at grooveessentials@tommyigoe.com. Hey, don't forget to wear earplugs, and clean underwear.

BIOGRAPHY

Tommy Igoe has been at the forefront of drumset performance and education for the last 20 years. Growing up in a musical home, he was drumming before he could walk and has never stopped. He won every local and regional competition in the New York City area during his high school years while simultaneously studying drumset and piano. Also, during these years, Tommy joined the famed Bayonne Bridgemen drumline of the early 1980's where he experienced some of his most cherished musical moments.

At the age of 18, he embarked on his first global tour with the Glenn Miller Orchestra and from that point his career took off. The next 15 years saw Tommy performing with Lauryn Hill, New York Voices, Leni Stern, Dave Grusin, Patti Austin, Blood Sweat and Tears, Darlene Love and Stanley Jordan amongst many others. Towards the end of this period, he became a permanent member of folk-rock legend Art Garfunkel's band, touring worldwide for more than nine years.

As his performing career flourished, Tommy simultaneously focused on education, teaching privately when possible and serving as an adjunct professor of jazz studies at Rutgers University. It was during this time that his unique methodology for drumset education was cultivated and he soon became known as one of the premier drumset educators in the world, performing clinics and master classes at schools, universities and drum-shops across the globe.

In 1997, the music team creating the Broadway musical version of The Lion King approached Tommy to help write the drumset book for what would be a groundbreaking theatrical event. Taking elements of traditional African percussion and blending them with the modern drumset had never been attempted on Broadway before and what resulted took Broadway and the entire music theatre community by storm, winning multiple Tony and Grammy awards. More than 10 Lion King companies in 8 different countries are currently performing Tommy's drumset book around the world. Presently, he serves as conductor with the original Broadway company of The Lion King in New York City.

In 2002, Tommy joined forces with Rob Wallis and Paul Siegel of Hudson Music to bring his teaching philosophies to DVD starting with the acclaimed *Getting Started On Drums*. Shortly thereafter, the best-selling Groove Essentials DVD was created, which received rave reviews and a demand from customers for a play-along version incorporating all the music from the DVD. In response to these adamant requests, *The Groove Essentials Play-Along* was born.

Tommy has played on well over 1000 commercials, soundtracks and film scores and is currently based in the New York City suburbs where he was born and raised. In addition to his weekly Big-Band gig at the legendary Birdland jazz club, you can see his complete itinerary at www.tommyigoe.com. Tommy Igoe plays Vic Firth sticks and mallets, Zildjian cymbals, Yamaha drums, Evans drumheads, L.P. percussion and Rhythm Tech accessories exclusively.

tommy igoe's
Great Hands for a
lifetime
Featuring the Lifetime Warmup™

A no-nonsense guide to hand technique that uses the best-selling Groove Essentials™ approach to achieve incredible results that last a lifetime!

Great Hands for a lifetime offers a realistic, practical approach that will unlock your potential and protect your hands through years of drumming. Developed to improve the strength, speed, stamina, comfort and control of every drummer, the 4-hour DVD features:

GREAT HANDS FOR A LIFETIME FEATURING THE LIFETIME WARMUP™ INCLUDES:

- *Matched and Traditional Grip*
- *Fulcrum Concepts*
- *Rebound Strokes*
- *Accents*
- *Single/Double-Stroke Check Patterns*
- *The Five Families of Rudiments Group Exercise Routines*
- *Lifetime Warmup™ Elements Explained*

- *Three Levels of Lifetime Warmup™ Demoed with Group*
- *MP3s for on-the-go practicing*
- *57-page eBook with extra practice material*
- *Wall-sized poster and compact fold-out guide*
- *Interview with Sonny Igoe*

Good technique requires maintenance! The *Lifetime Warmup*™ is how it's done!

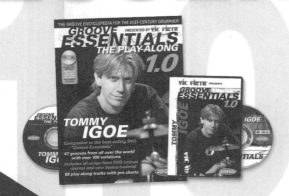